Unsuited

Unsuited

How We Can Reject Conventional Career Advice and Find Empowerment

By

Ryan Clements

SENSE PUBLISHERS
ROTTERDAM / BOSTON / TAIPEI

A C.I.P. record for this book is available from the Library of Congress.

ISBN 978-94-6209-645-5 (paperback)
ISBN 978-94-6209-646-2 (hardback)
ISBN 978-94-6209-647-9 (e-book)

Published by: Sense Publishers,
P.O. Box 21858, 3001 AW Rotterdam, The Netherlands
https://www.sensepublishers.com/

Printed on acid-free paper

To Joe:
Thank you for inspiring and teaching me.
I miss you.

Contents

Why This Book?

Are We Empowered?

My outlook on life is very different from what it used to be. I no longer wake up each morning to a sigh, and a heavy and slow departure from my bed. I no longer dread Sunday nights, the end of a vacation, or take that extra half an hour at lunch when I can get away with it. I now wake up each day ready to do my work, my core values aligned with my goals and life's purpose, and I often work late into the night, not because I have to, but because I want to.

I once hoped that my workday would go by quickly, so that I could escape to a hobby or entertainment. Now I wish the days would slow down. Now I rarely get done all the things that I want to do, but each day I am still fulfilled. Now I try to make each day my masterpiece. Now I am pulled by my dreams, not held hostage by my fears. Now I feel like I am doing exactly what I was meant to do. Now I feel a sense of control, a sense of engagement, a sense of participation in my life, and a sense of feeling alive. Now I am free. Now I am empowered.

How did I make this change? I had re-educate myself. Despite eight years of post-secondary schooling, and the obtaining of multiple degrees, including a law degree, I was not educated. I realized that I knew *nothing* about what would actually bring me fulfillment. I had memorized a string of facts and unrelated information. I had gained knowledge. I had refined my abilities to think and reason critically. I had said the right things to the right people at the right time, but I had assumed that fulfillment was a byproduct of achievement.

I assumed that if I just kept achieving (regardless of the nature of the achievement) that I would find the fulfillment that I was seeking. For me the prize was the purpose, not the journey or the pursuit. I believed that all I had to do was secure prestigious degrees, land a high paying and secure job and I would be happy, so I did it all, only to find myself in the darkest moments of depression and personal discouragement.

This book is not a book about being successful and getting rich. This book is about tapping the authenticity and creativity that is inside of all of us, and summoning the courage to launch it to the world. This book will empower, accommodate, and advise us to make a change that will give our working life a sense of meaning. I will make the case that we are better off pursuing careers that are dedicated to mastery, continual improvement and psychological flow, rather than careers motivated by fear, a hope for financial security, and the desire for social prestige.

We are all creators. How or if we unleash our creativity, is up to us. The ability to nurture, cultivate, and ultimately share our unique voice is a personal choice. But it is a choice that many of us don't make. We don't make this choice because it is scary, and sometimes risky, and many of us simply don't know how to tap into the creativity that is inside of us.

As a result, we rationalize and settle in life. We do this because we can secure a "safe" job, and a "respectable" level of financial security, and protect ourselves against exposure to pain. We say, "I'm nothing special," or "I should just be grateful for what I have," but deep down inside we hope for something more, and we believe that we are capable of doing unique things. We know what it is that makes us yearn. It is very personal, and it is revealed to us when we see someone else producing it, when someone else is living the life we want. It has absolutely nothing to do with acquiring more possessions or gaining more status in the world. We yearn to create like they are creating, produce like they are producing, and feel alive in an authentic way.

To curb the craving we turn to distractions. We look at the "working hours" of the day as a necessary evil in our life. We do what we need to do to "pay the bills." We live for the weekend or for our next vacation. We sleep walk through life, without even attempting to live deeply. We don't attempt risk, and we don't confront our fears. We substitute a life of inner substance and creation for one of external recognition and the acquisition of material possessions. We pass the time with distraction, entertainment, and the pursuit of goals that aren't personally meaningful, such as making more money. But we are confused when these goals never seem to fully satisfy. Does any of this sound familiar? Has this occurred in your life? It has for me. It was my life, and I had to change it.

For many years I lived this way. I pursued a career that had no meaning to me, other than money and a misguided sense of prestige. I thought that I was actually being rational and prudent by making decisions that led me to a career that I had no interest spending the remainder of my life in, a career that led to anxiety and depression. In order to become empowered, in order for things to change, I had to change. I had to accept responsibility for the life I chose, and then I had to make new choices that were in line with what I really valued.

We are born into a world of demands, many of which conflict. We are taught in school to seek the "right answers," and to be compliant and obedient, but "right" is a matter of subjection. Fear of failure encourages safe choices, even if the safe choices ultimately lead to an unfulfilling destination. Fear stifles experimentation and makes creatively impotent. For many of us, the perceived cost of failure is just too high, so when making choices relating to our life and career we seek a path that will provide financially, not one that will fulfill. Then we find other pursuits to fill our time instead of creating, producing and sharing that special gift that is inside of us.

Our standard is the mythical "successful" person, and this is the measure by which society judges us. It is also the measure by which we judge ourselves. Why do we need to succeed, and under whose rules do we measure failure? What is enough success? Why do we measure the value of our entire life by what we possess, and the titles that we maintain? These rules do not make us happy, and we don't have to live by them. Failure can be empowering. Success can lead to anxiety and depression. We can change the rules. We can create our own rules.

Making changes requires a "re-education" process, because our formal education gave us an "employee" mindset. It conditioned us to be passive, obedient, to resist risk, and to feel a sense of entitlement because of our education, not because of the value we are giving to the world. In Chapter One I discuss our history of schooling, why we go to school, and how school conditions us not to be creators. This conditioning might lead to job security, but it can be a major handicap to fulfillment. We need to discover what makes us tick inside, and what our unique core values are. Once we determine these, we need to align our goals, and our daily actions, with these values.

To become empowered I had to change my story about the world. We all have our own stories, our own narratives about the world, and how it works, I had to rewrite mine to find fulfillment. I had to understand that I had been chasing achievement to find fulfillment, but that fulfillment wasn't the prize of success. Success only produced more longing for success. It was a vicious cycle. Something had to give to break the cycle and provide fulfillment. I discovered that I wasn't that motivated by money or status. I wanted my life to mean something, and I longed for freedom and the ability to create and add value to others.

I realized that I was operating under a set of assumptions and rules about the world that didn't work for me. So I rejected much of the conventional career wisdom that I had spent the first ten years of my adult life refining. I accepted full personal responsibility for my choices, and realized that I was not a victim, and that I had the power to control the outcome of my life, if I could overcome my fear. For me this meant walking away from a safe and prestigious career to pursue a path of entrepreneurialism—a world where my reward would come from my ability to provide value to others.

To find empowerment I chose to embrace life as a series of experiments, all of which could lead to my own empowerment, education and instruction. I re-wrote my story about education, away from a results based mindset (obtaining degrees), to one that was about process, learning and continuation. I overcame my fear of failure and criticism. I liberated myself from the chains of consistency, and learned not to be held hostage by the choices of my past. I re-educated myself to not be concerned with how I looked to others, or how a decision would affect my resume or career trajectory, but rather to look internally and make decisions that aligned with my core values. I then summoned the courage to be my true self, and pursue my own unique path, even if that path meant walking down the mountain I had climbed.

To achieve empowerment it was very important to understand that there was risk in every aspect of life, and that everything had a cost, even career options that were conventionally secure. However, risk was something that I could manage, it was not something to run from. It was actually a great asset and a blessing. I embraced the notion that adding real and genuine value to others was far more important than recording notches on my success record, and that adding value would outweigh career distinctions and strategically motivated relationships. Society's rewards were not the purpose of life alone. Rewards alone would not lead to my personal fulfillment. I learned to find joy in the journey. I learned to embrace each day and make it my masterpiece. I learned to seek mastery, not just because of what I would get from it, or who it would impress, but rather because there was fulfillment intrinsically in pursuing mastery. I learned that the art of fulfillment was the art of immersion, independent of external rewards.

This book is about empowerment and what it takes to arrive at this state. It will help us when we become discontent with our daily reality, and wonder if it is all that life will present. When we look back at our formal educational decisions and wonder how we got to the place where we are right now. It's for all of us who wonder why we aren't fulfilled, despite doing what is generally accepted, and regarded as prudent and practical.

It is for those of us who believe that the path to fulfillment can be undertaken without significant risk if the game is played correctly, and who would love a change in our career or life, but feel stuck, and don't know the steps to take. It is for all of us who continue to hypnotize ourselves with the false belief that it is too risky to change right now, and that the timing just isn't right, or that material comforts can compensate for a lack of day-to-day fulfillment.

This book is also for those of us who are just starting out in our career. I know that we can chase our passions, if we just give ourselves permission. Avoiding risk, and taking a conventionally "safe" path is not a badge of honor that we will be proud to wear one day. It is a massive risk in and of itself. The world has changed. There are options and choices available to us that never previously existed. It is critical in our life that we obtain, and continue to seek, an education. But education is not limited to the parchments that hang on our wall. The traditional path of securing the degree and landing the high paying job, will not guarantee our fulfillment. We can be fulfilled, we deserve to be happy, and this book will provide a map to that destination.

Checkpoint: Are We Empowered?

- ✓ Are we on a career path that is personally meaningful?

- ✓ Do we wonder sometimes how we got here, and what to do about it?

- ✓ Are we willing to commit ourselves to mastering the path we're on?

- ✓ Do we wake up each day with a sense of excitement and urgency?

- ✓ Are we giving our best creative work to the world?

- ✓ Are we empowered?

Chapter One

Learning and Then Having to Unlearn

The Sugar Beet Field, and My Plan to Transcend It

It was a cool, wet morning, early in the summer. My job was to move irrigation pipes at our family's sugar beet farm. We didn't have the luxury of irrigation pivots; ours were the manual wheel move sprinklers that needed to be moved fifteen rows every five hours. My younger brother Curtis and I walked in our gumboots from our house to the field where the wheel mover was located. That day I had a distinct impression—I wanted to be somebody in life. Not here—somewhere different. I thought of large buildings and men in suits. I thought about being "important" and "smart." I didn't know how, I didn't know where, I didn't even know what, I just knew that I wanted more than what was in that field.

I grew up in a family that loved me deeply, with parents who would give anything to ensure my happiness and success. I had coaches and youth leaders from my church that cared about my welfare. I had teachers who were interested in my development. I had every advantage as a child. I didn't receive pressure from anyone to be anything. My ambitions and motivations were driven from within. As I grew I formed my own assumptions about what it would take to transcend the field.

It was never expected of me to take over the farm. However, it wasn't encouraged either. Formal education was encouraged. There was a general belief, both in the small town that I grew up in, and my family, that people who had formal college and graduate level education had a significant advantage, and status, over those who didn't. It was also believed that the pinnacle of education was being a "professional," such as a doctor, a lawyer, a dentist or an accountant—these were the people who had the nice homes, the nice cars, and took the good vacations. So I believed that my education had to translate into practical application and money. That was what many people thought, and since I wanted out of the field, it seemed like the best path.

As a result, I believed that pragmatic education was my ticket to money, freedom and success. It became critical that I did well in school, that way I could attend a good university, and get into a good profession. To me, formalized education, ideally with the end goal of becoming a professional was a symbol of status, a badge of intelligence, and a path to security and comfort. I came, on my own accord, to firmly believe that formal education was the answer; formal education was the solution, not just for me, but also for anyone who wanted more in life. A successful man was an educated man. Of course, at that time, I didn't know there were multiple *educations* in life.

Until I obtained a professional, post-graduate degree, I had done little, if any, research on how our current schooling system came into existence. More importantly I hadn't stopped to consider why the educational system was designed the way it was. I had just accepted its existence, and assumed that my ability to successfully navigate its methods was at the heart of my future well-being. In retrospect, understanding how "education" came to be was an important step in my own emancipation from this education.

Just How Did We Become Educated?

Becoming empowered is a process. Part of that process is to understand how we arrived in a state of non-empowerment. By learning our own histories, we begin to understand our stories.

In ancient Greece, philosophers would provide lectures in the streets of Athens.[1] During the European dark ages, Christianity strictly controlled most formal education, including access to almost all written materials; and as a result, during this period, many people lived and eventually died without obtaining any schooling. Learning was a function of necessity, religion, myth, or curiosity. It was hardly institutionalized outside of the church. We learned what we needed to know in order to literally survive (for example how to farm or grow food, how to hunt, how to operate the family business or means of livelihood, and how to defend ourselves from thieves and intruders). Anything above that was usually in the nature of spiritualism, mysticism, or cultural ritual. At times we were curious, so we sought out the mysteries that aroused our interest, but this didn't take place institutionally. We learned by experience, stories, individual experimentation, and informal mentoring.

Thought leaders like Martin Luther and Isaac Newton worked to remove scripture from school curriculum, and tirelessly crusaded to give science equal footing with religion.[2] Yet, the modern day "school" was not designed for the purpose of inspiration. Schools were designed to teach religious ethics, dogmatic obedience and most importantly strict discipline. Schools were created to build obedient workers—workers that would supply the means of labor to the ever-changing institutions of power—divine, governmental or corporate.

North America's oldest school, the Boston Latin School, along with three of the first Ivy League Schools: Dartmouth, Harvard and Yale, were founded by Puritans, the radical protestant sect who weren't fond of smiling and had a certain proclivity to round up witches. The idyllic "one room schoolhouse" was a Puritan creation, so were some of the earliest laws mandating schooling for children.

Author Zander Sherman in his book, *The Curiosity of School, Education and the Dark Side of Enlightenment*, details the Puritan's influence on an early Massachusetts law, which oddly enough, came about solely as an attempt to thwart the devil:

---

1 Sherman, Zander. *The Curiosity of School: Education and the Dark Side of Enlightenment.* Toronto: Penguin Group (Canada), 2012. Print.

2 Sherman 4.

Puritans were looking for a way to inculcate their children with Puritan values, and school arrived at the right time. In 1646, Massachusetts legislated the Old Deluder Law, which asserted that it was the chief objective 'of that old deluder, Satan, to keep men from the knowledge of the scriptures'. To counter the ways of the evil trickster, the law required every town with fifty families to hire a schoolmaster, and every town with a hundred families to manage a grammar school at its own expense. The Old Deluder Law was the first time any attempt had been made to regulate education in the state of Massachusetts.[3]

The confederation of the United States of America generated a movement to unify and homogenize a "system" of schooling that would benefit the newly formed nation. The system that was ultimately chosen was not a "uniquely" American creation—it was based on a Prussian model having been devised and refined by an Eighteenth century philosopher, and Immanuel Kant devotee, Johann Fichte. An ambitious young professor and writer, Fichte desired for his philosophy to change the world. His initial target: the German educational system. Sherman writes,

> After returning to Berlin in 1807, Fichte began delivering a series of speeches in the amphitheater of the Academy of the Sciences...Addressing the emotionally dejected audience of former Prussians, Fichte professed to know why Prussia had lost to Napoleon—and moreover, how it could bounce back. 'In a word, it is a total change of the existing system of education that I propose as the sole means of preserving the existence of the German nation.'[4]

Fichte's methods were based on de-emphasizing individuality and free will, thereby molding a nation into a unified body. Sherman continues,

> These were, to say the least, radical ideas. As Bertrand Russell summarized Fichte from this period: 'Education should aim at destroying free will, so that, after pupils have left school they shall be incapable, throughout the rest of their lives, of thinking or acting otherwise than as their schoolmasters would have wished.' Public, legally enforced education would substitute identity, free thought, and creativity with, as Fichte put it, 'a fixed and unchangeable machine.'[5]

3   Sherman 4.

4   Sherman 19.

5   Sherman 20.

Horace Mann, often referred to as *the father of the common school,* was a key figure in American modern education. Mann was highly influenced by the Prussian educational system. Mann invented the "common" school model (a precursor to modern day public schools), helped to create the first State Board of Education in America (Massachusetts) and was also instrumental in implementing compulsory schools. Mann's *Annual Reports,* commentaries and critiques of the educational model, which were drafted while he served as secretary to the Massachusetts Board of Education, are considered some of the most influential works in American educational history.[6]

Mann didn't study educational philosophy in University. He was a lawyer and a politician. However, when personal tragedy struck (Mann's first wife Charlotte died at a very young age from tuberculosis) Mann withdrew from public life and professional law practice. A very articulate debater, Mann seemed destined to influence others, his second wife Mary Peabody Mann would later write that he was "*born to sway men.*"[7] Mann's persuasive abilities are what landed him the job as secretary to the Massachusetts Board of Education, a position that he would hold for over a decade where he would influence the course of American educational reform. These abilities were critical, as the Board's mandate was to convince the diverse and immigrant rich Massachusetts population base that a system of common and centralized schooling was necessary.

Mann's primary means of influence were his *Annual Reports,* which would include status reports of the various state's school districts as well as commentary and recommendations for strengthening the schools. In his reports Mann advocated measures like controlling the textbooks that were used, as well as influencing the curriculum (for example he sought to limit, or ban, textbooks that presented alternative world views or were conflicting to Mann's own values).

Mann's relationship with, and influence from, fellow educational reformer Charles Brooks led him to petition the House Committee for the establishment of two "normal schools" in Massachusetts. Brooks had extensive knowledge of the Prussian system and felt strongly about the superiority of

---

6   Sherman 25.

7   Sherman 34.

their methods, and he was determined to introduce their system to America.[8] Normal schools (a form of teacher training college) were a mainstay in the Prussian system and were an important development in the establishment of "teaching" as a recognized and respected profession.

In 1844, while on his honeymoon to his second wife Mary Peabody, Mann took the time to visit Berlin and see for himself the nature of the Prussian schooling system. This trip would solidify his resolve to integrate their methods into his state and the American nation. Sherman notes,

> Though he was finished half the reports that he would author on the adoption of the Prussian system, when the Manns arrived in Berlin, it was the first time Mann had actually seen a Prussian school. Still, he felt Prussia stood 'pre-eminent among the nations of Europe in regard to the quantity and quality of education'.

Mann's impact on the common mode of schooling is unmistakable. It became his life's work and central meaning. He truly believed that he was changing society for the better by helping to usher a Prussian system in America. Twelve years before the Massachusetts Board of Education legislated compulsory schooling he wrote, "*this institution is the greatest discovery ever made by man.… we repeat it, the common school is the greatest discovery ever made by man.*"[9]

The modern educational model was not founded on the principles of individual experimentation and freedom. It was not designed as a lab to stimulate creativity. It was designed for the "masses," not for us as individuals. It was driven much more by the principles of obedience, conformance, and compulsion than it was on unique, individualized and subjective learning. Mann actually garnered mass support for schools by guaranteeing that he could create docile and obedient workers by using his formula for schooling. I didn't know this at the time. How could I have known? I trusted that if I put my faith in the "system," everything would work out fine.

Enter Fredrick Taylor, widely regarded as the *Father of Scientific Management*. If Mann's model was the "cake" in our current educational system, then Taylor's philosophies have become the cherry on top. Fredrick Winslow

---

8   Sherman 32.

9   Sherman 36.

Taylor, was born on March 20, 1865, to an established Quaker family in Pennsylvania. His father was a wealthy lawyer. He had aspirations to follow in his father's footsteps, but he struggled with poor eyesight. As a result, he chose to become an apprentice machinist and he took up work with a pump-manufacturing company in Philadelphia. After his apprenticeship he became a laborer for a steel works company, later climbing the responsibility ladder to become research director and finally chief engineer for the company.

As his responsibilities grew, he found himself as a manager of human laborers. Taylor became obsessed with the notion of efficiency in industrial production. Over time he developed his own philosophies relating to maximizing human capital through labor, and he used his ideas to develop a lucrative business as a consultant, essentially creating the "management consulting" industry as it exists today.[10]

Taylor believed that a company should actively develop employees for specific tasks, rather than allowing them to train themselves. People were to be "mechanisms" in the factory, not independent thinking, and creative individuals working together for a common good. He believed that each worker should have detailed instructions and supervision in the performance of a specific task, and that there was to be a division between management and workers, such that management planned and supervised the work, and workers performed it.[11] He had intellectual distain for the workers, and once suggested to a congressional committee that they were too "stupid" to comprehend the science behind what they were doing.[12] Management was planning work (intellectual) and labor was manual work (non-intellectual, execution of tasks).

Taylor's philosophies were widely adopted and his influence spread rapidly. There is no question that Taylor's methods led to efficiency improvements, and increased profitability, but it had a dark side. The pace of work became accelerated, autonomy restricted, skilled craftsmanship destroyed

---

10 Merkle, Judith A. *Management and Ideology: The Legacy Of The International Scientific Management Movement.* Berkley: University of California Press, 1980. Print.

11 Wren, Daniel. *The Evolution of Management Thought.* New York: John Wiley and Sons, Inc., 1987. Print.

12 Montgomery, David. *The Fall of the House of Labor: The Workplace, the State, and American Labor Activism, 1865-1925.* New York: Press Syndicate of the University of Cambridge, 1987. Print.

leading to lower product quality, and the identity of workers was under-mined.[13] People became reduced to machines in a factory. There was no mastery in a craft, only efficiency, productivity and profit.

Just like in the factories and companies, Taylor's methods and philoso-phies have been widely accepted in the workings of our schools. Teachers are the managers, controlling and supervising the tasks to be performed. Stu-dents are the workers, and are expected to follow, with precision, the com-mands given. Standardization, efficiency and control are paramount goals. There are even bells, just like the whistles in a factory. Autonomy, individual experimentation and creatively are not widely cultivated, other than by the efforts of exceptional teachers who resist the status quo. Students become proficient at executing tasks and being obedient, thus making them mod-el workers to enter society. Because of the philosophies of Fredrick Taylor, schools have become proficient training grounds for entrance into the fac-tory of life. However, it doesn't equip them with the necessary skills to find, or maintain, fulfillment. It equips them to have a job. To follow orders, and to execute instructions, just like Taylor's factory model.

The First Cracks in My Paradigm

It was my sophomore year, and I was an undergraduate economics major. I was taking an introductory macroeconomics class and I was engaged with the subject, particularly the question of whether active government policy actually mattered, or whether it was just the perception of action that moved the markets. I was reading widely outside of the class syllabus, trying to find an answer to this question. It was engaging to me. I wanted to know how the world really worked. I had a real enthusiasm for learning, it wasn't just about the grade for me, I found the discovery process intrinsically rewarding. In my research I discovered that my question wasn't fully settled. There was evi-dence, and support, on both sides of the argument, and no definitive answer.

This was a new discovery for me. Up until that point school was simply memorizing what was in a book and then regurgitating it up at test time. I felt like I had mastered this process in high school, and my grades reflected

---

13   Waring, Stephen P. *Taylorism Transformed: Scientific Management Theory since 1945*. Chapel Hill and London: University of North Carolina Press; 1991. Print.

it, but now I had the scary epiphany that perhaps there wasn't always a right answer. If this were the case, then I would have to take a position. If I took a position, what if my position was different from my teacher's position? How would my grades be impacted? How would my future be impacted? Could I question my own education? Could I challenge a teacher?

This was my literal thought process at nineteen. I believed so strongly that my future rested on my ability to get top grades, so the unsettling reality of an uncontrollable variable in a game I thought I had mastered left me very anxious. What would this mean for my system? What would happen when my position put me at odds with my teacher? Would I have the courage to stick to my position, even if it meant a compromise to my grades? What if I was right on an issue but the teacher didn't accept my position? Or worse yet, what if there was no right answer, but the teacher controlled the grade? How was I to act then?

One day my professor addressed the concept that I had been researching. Now this particular class, and this particular professor, unfortunately characterizes the reality of many undergraduate classes: a distant teacher who has very little interest in the students and the rudimentary course content; and, distant students who have very little interest in the teacher and the course (other than getting the requisite credits to apply to their degree program).

Our professor delivered each class in a formal lecture format. Participation was not mandated, and it definitely wasn't encouraged. He was our preacher, we were his congregation. He used to pace back and forth, delivering the gospel of introductory macroeconomics to a disinterested crowd. As far as we were concerned, his words were the factual truth, and all we needed to know about this particular subject.

Despite his mode of delivery, I found his lectures engaging. I was engaged because I had an interest in the topic. I actually cared about what he was teaching. I took copious notes. I thought about what he was saying and I did research to find proof of what he was talking about. I read widely outside of the material, not because I had to, but because it was interesting to me. So on that formative day, early in the semester, after a particularly interesting lecture (at least to me), I summoned my enthusiasm, and courage, and decided that I would go and introduce myself to the teacher. I wanted him to see me as a keen student, but more importantly I wanted to discuss the topic of the day's lecture because I had actually read something that disputed what he was saying (and more than one source for that matter). Truthfully I thought that what he had said made less sense (practically) than what I had read.

His interaction with me was a defining moment in my formal educational experience (even though I continued my post-secondary training for many years after). It left me with a healthy sense of reality, but also a lingering distaste in my mouth. This professor summarily dismissed me. As I introduced myself I felt that he looked at me with distain at the worst, and clear disinterest at the best. I know I was a second year undergraduate student and not one of his prized doctorate students. I know that I had very little to offer him personally. But I was amazed at how uncomfortable I felt during and after our encounter.

I introduced myself. He said simply, "Hi." Then I asked my question in a way that I thought would trigger a healthy conversation. I started with, "I have been reading, and it seems like there are other positions on this issue." He bluntly dismissed my self-directed research, and me for that matter. He stated that my position was wrong; that what he had covered in the lecture was correct. He didn't engage, he didn't inquire as to where I gained my contradictory information and he didn't encourage me to look deeper. He flatly indicated that he was right and that I was wrong, and that there was nothing further to discuss. To this day I guarantee that within seconds of hearing my name he had already forgotten it.

I left that encounter feeling confused. I didn't have the contradictory references with me, so I couldn't pull out support to refute him, and besides I didn't want to fight with my Professor. It wasn't my intention to show up my teacher. Maybe that was what he thought—that I was just some "know-it-all" student who was out of his league. But that wasn't my intention at all. I was like an intellectual puppy—excited and interested but naïve. I just knew that the issue wasn't as black and white as he was leading me to believe. However, through the interaction I knew that there was a very clear power dynamic at play in school, and that my grades could be jeopardized if I insisted on pushing my position. Especially in this type of mass student, multiple-choice format style, introductory class.

Looking back, the exchange happened quite quickly—a student with enthusiasm tries to engage a disinterested professor. The professor interprets the exchange as a student trying to challenge his intellectual domain. The professor uses the power structure to maintain order. There it was for me. That was my new epiphany. School wasn't about becoming smart or learning. It was a game, with rules and rewards. I had to learn to master the rules if I wanted to get the rewards.

Before this I had always believed that my teachers acted in my best interest—the interest of making me smart, and helping me to learn. Now I knew that subjective biases were possible, and that there wasn't always a right answer, and that the teacher controlled my grade. At the time I felt that if they controlled my grade they also controlled my future. I have since completely disregarded (fortunately) this belief. But at the time I felt that I needed a formal educational endorsement in order to succeed and find fulfillment. Given this new variable I now had to adapt in order to survive.

I readily admit that not all of my teachers acted like this Professor. However, without a doubt, in both of my post-secondary degrees, Economics and Law, an engaging teacher, who was more interested in teaching than research and their own career projection, was absolutely the exception, not the norm. There were a number of good ones that I was exposed to over the course of my educational experience. I am grateful for this because I know that there are distinct minorities who are resisting the institutional pressures that are so real on academics: publish or perish; research is more important than teaching; and herd the students through the course content. The institutional pressures have a trickle down effect on students who leave this "factory" disenchanted with their expensive experience, and wondering what the whole point of it was (other than a necessity to gain a job—society's sorting mechanism).

For me, adaptation soon turned to success as I put this new variable into play in all my classes going forward. Each class that I took was for a purpose, the purpose was to get the credit with top marks, the credit got me the degree, and the degree with top honors got me the life that I thought at the time would bring me peace and happiness. I knew that in order to succeed, not only did I have to learn what the Professor wanted me to learn, but also

I needed to synthesize it in a way that they liked (and agreed with), so that I could recite it back to them like they were writing the test themselves.

Playing the Game Took Its Toll and Changed Who I Was, But Not for the Better

My strategy worked flawlessly and I was able to rise to high honors as an undergraduate, and carry that momentum into a similar record in law school. I was in the top 5% of my class in both disciplines. The world was now in front of me. I would have the pick of the jobs in the country, and I did. I thought everything was finally coming together. I was feeling validated, this was the path: excel in school (even if it meant playing a game) and the world would open up. Little did I know how much my worldview would change within six years of graduating from law school.

While I was in college, and playing the game, I took great pleasure in my ability. I would often quietly brag about it to others—how I had "figured out the system" and how school was just a game. My advice to others was simple: learn the rules of the game. Figure out exactly what the professor wanted to hear and give it to them. Find out their position, their perspective, their biases, and their inclinations. Play to their egos if necessary, not in a "sucking up" way, but in a way that made them understand that you really knew the material, from their perspective, through their interpretation. Then, when called upon, produce a product with such clarity that when they read your paper, essay, or test, they themselves would feel like they wrote it.

This strategy worked tremendously, and my grades reflected it, I was a star student. Participation in class was only necessary if the teacher rewarded participation. When I found this type of class I would be the top participant. In classes where participation wasn't rewarded I took great pleasure in quietly analyzing the teacher, reading their work, going to talk to them after hours, getting to know them, finding out what their research interests were. Then I would focus my efforts in that class on the particular emphasis they placed on certain concepts. It is amazing that this strategy consistently worked in every class, both undergraduate and law school. To this day I laugh at how easy it was to get consistent top marks when I took this approach.

I was beginning to feel a great struggle within. I felt like a shadow of my true self. I was never cheating. I never engaged in "academic dishonest behavior" as defined by the school, but I still felt like I was living an intellectual lie because I would never let my own thoughts or feelings be known if they were contrary to those of my Professor. I was living solely for the rewards, and the intrinsic value of the learning was lost.

I was developing strong internal discontent, because I would read and learn and form opinions and beliefs, but when it came test time I would shrink. I would just parrot back to the teacher exactly what they wanted to hear, based on their opinions, perspective and biases, not mine. I would just go in, get the grade, and get out. My "learning" was comprised of my need to obtain a goal. But the goal started to lose meaning. By law school I was quite internally discouraged about how artificial I found the whole process. I was conditioning myself to respond this way because it produced results, and results were my focus. I felt that the ends justified the means, but I was starting to feel manipulative (which I now believe I was) and I was also tiring of the game, especially in law school where my own subjective interpretation of cases and legal reasoning was a daily occurrence.

I would often read a case and form an entirely different opinion of its interpretation, or the public policy implications that the case suggested, than my Professor; however, I knew that I would get a better grade in an exam or on a paper if I focused on their preferred position and then backed it up with a high volume of case research. I always envied the students who would take a strong opposing stand in class to a Professor. Deep down inside, I wished that I could be like them, but I had no incentive to change a process that was working so well. I thought that if I just got the grade it would all be worth it.

University started to feel like a giant factory that was pumping out human widgets to serve in various limited, and controlled, capacities in society. Like the methods advocated by Taylor, there was a divide between the teachers and the students. My role was simply to shut up and learn. I had to gain a skill set so that I could become employable. I told myself that if I had to be a widget then I would at least be one with comfy surroundings. I soon found myself at the end of an established road, and despite the completion of over eight years of post-secondary education, I felt like I really hadn't learned anything.

Worst of all, I was cynical. What was the whole point of this exercise? Why did I need society to bestow the title of intelligence on me? Was this the only path? Why did I think this was the only path? Why was having a degree, or multiple degrees, even necessary? Anyone could obtain one—if they had the money and the ability to understand and implement the game. That naïve, but intellectually enthusiastic, sophomore undergraduate had been replaced by a cold and calculating law grad. I had made it to the end of the road. Now my intention was to milk it for all it was worth. I felt like it was my earned right. I had done exactly what the system had mandated. Now it was time for my payday.

The contrarian students who would take on a Professor (in many cases to the detriment of their grades) and defend a position always inspired me, but it seemed to me that these students weren't populating the Dean's List— these weren't the students that were being heavily recruited by the prestigious law firms, nor were they the students who seemed to be landing the top paying jobs. I would literally tell myself, and my closest friends in law school that, "one day when I'm in practice I will take and defend my own unique positions. For now I just play the game." If I could just get through this, if I could just play the game until the end, I could obtain that golden ticket. I would have the prestigious law degree with honors. I would have the job offers with the swanky and high paying firms, I would have money and I would be happy. All but the latter would come true in my law career. For happiness, I had to first make a significant discovery and then develop the courage to make dramatic changes in my life. That is what the remainder of this book is about.

Bright Lights, Big City: Confusion Sets In

After law school, my first job was in Toronto with one of the most prestigious and high paying corporate law firms in Canada. I decided that I would make a name for myself in securities and mergers and acquisitions law. Despite a degree in economics, and having studied the securities in law school, I really knew nothing about what life would be like as a securities lawyer. I had read *Barbarians At The Gates, Liar's Poker,* watched *Wall Street,* and had started to romanticize investment-banking firms like KKR and Bain Capital.

I dreamed of life as a "corporate raider" making millions at the center of the universe. I saw the world I was entering into as one of high stakes corporate takeovers and charismatic business people. It seemed fresh and exciting, and also seemed to fit my newly formed cynical, yet calculating personality. I was like a nouveau Gordon Gekko (minus the corruption). Come to think about it, I was exactly like Bud Fox, willing to do what it took to get ahead.

It was important for me to get a feel for the social landscape at my new firm so that I could implement my strategic plan. The problem was that the specifics, or endgame, of that plan was never clear to me. I had a general desire to be recognized as a "successful" person, and I thought that being rich was better than being poor. I wanted to be acknowledged by others; especially my family and friends back home. I wanted to be acknowledged by my law Professors and fellow students. I wanted to be known as a person who had "made it." I wanted people to talk about my success. I now clearly understand that all these wants were driven by insecurity, but I masked the insecurity through massive ambition. I was a man possessed.

There was a culture present in law school that bigger was better. The large law firms were the ones who were sponsoring the moot court and negotiations competitions amongst the students, providing summer research fellowships, and receiving named classrooms and wings in the law school. It was a matter of wide discussion which students secured summer associate positions at which firms. There were stacks of free industry publications throughout the law school where the large law firms took out full-page ads to remind us of how important they were. Recruiters highlighted the perks: the money, the fancy gym memberships, the courtside seats, the nice restaurants and big deals. If we made it with them, we were going to be important people in the world.

The generally accepted wisdom in law school was to get the best grades so that we could secure the best paying, and most prestigious job possible. We had to start big, not small. This was the path to security and prosperity. It seemed that no one ever suggested following what we liked, or what we could see ourselves doing for the rest of our life. It was the large firms that dominated the in-school interviews. It was rare to see a student openly disregard a large law firm to pursue a passion driven interest or alternative career venture. Just as I had left my small hometown believing that that the world of higher education was the only road, I left law school feeling that it was big firm or nothing for me.

I never stopped to ask myself whether I actually wanted to be a big firm lawyer, or even what a big firm lawyer actually did? Oddly enough the question never really occurred to me, just as the question of whether I really needed all this formal education had never really occurred to me. It just happened without hesitation or analysis. Never did I stop to wonder if I was climbing a mountain that would mean nothing to me when I reached its apex. Nor did I stop to question whether there was an apex at all, or what the whole point of the struggle was. I never did what I wanted to do. I didn't even know what I wanted. I was chasing one carrot after the next. But each time I caught it, it didn't satisfy me. I didn't care about the reward.

After a year at my first firm I took a job with another international corporate law firm doing the same thing. It was essentially the same firm with a different name. The same type of work, the same environment, and the same type of social dynamics, and after a relatively short amount of time I formulated a number of distinct conclusions about my life and future as a corporate securities lawyer.

First, there was a vast separation between the junior lawyers and the firm partners. Although the recruiters and human resources staff at both firms told me to model the partners, and do what they told me to do, dress like they dressed, act like they acted, it was very clear to me that there was a large divide between us, and that most of the new lawyers would never become partners. Truthfully, very few of us even wanted it. Even though we would attend many of the same firm social functions and networking events (when we were invited) I clearly noticed the disparity. It was obvious.

One experience dramatically reinforced this divide for me. Along with a couple other junior associates, I had been working for a number of months on a fairly routine takeover. However to me, the deal had huge significance, I had really taken leadership in the drafting of the deal documents. As a young associate I really took pride in the transaction because it felt like it was mine. There was limited oversight on a partner level, other than the compensatory review of the deal documents, and ensuring our work had passed the requisite level of competence so as to avoid material error.

I was operating under the assumption that an associate was an integral and respected part of the transaction; without me, this deal may not happen. I was diligent in preparing the closing of the transaction, pulling an all-nighter the night before the closing day, to ensure that all our documents were appropriately drafted and complete, and the board room was immaculately prepared; so when the executives came in to sign, everything would go without a hitch. I definitely expected some recognition from my efforts in going the extra mile.

When the closing day came I was a ghost in the boardroom. I was so excited, so proud, yet so naïve. Not a single partner took the time to introduce me to the key executives on both sides of the transaction. Once the champagne glasses were drained and the partners headed out for their post closing dinner engagement, I was back in the boardroom cleaning up the paper and preparing closing folders. I chalked this up as an anomaly, I hadn't heard experiences with my peers in big law firms throughout North America. But there was a caste system in these big firms. We had to pay our dues.

Paying our dues meant being devoid of personal control and a personal life, until we ascended the ranks within the power structure. Our Blackberry was our master, it could summon us at any time and we were required to respond. The proverbial carrot and stick were ever present. We were reminded by people at the firm, our family members and the general media, of how bad the economy was, how tough the job market was, and how much risk there was "out there." We were conditioned to believe that risk was something to be avoided, instead of intelligently understood. We were lucky to be there.

There were the hopes of the pay, the partnership, the prestige, the corner office, and the lifetime of financial security. We would get these if we paid our dues and did our time. I had no problem with the concept of paying "dues." I was raised on the belief that everything had a cost, and nothing was free. So I expected to have to pay dues to achieve a reward. At first, the rewards were the sole motivator: the prestige, the money, and the external signs of success. However, I realized over time that the rewards were becoming less meaningful. Also, I never entered the profession to perfect the craft. I didn't have an intrinsic love of what I was doing. So when the rewards started losing their meaning, I found myself in a dark place, with no motivation to continue.

Also, I was sacrificing all that was meaningful to me to the firm. I had no time for my wife or my kids. If I was home when they were awake, I was so exhausted that I didn't have the energy to actively participate in their lives. I wanted to sit and watch TV, or sit in the steam room. The commuting time was devastating as well. I used to sit and look at everyone's face. Everyone seemed so discontent, so unhappy. I had no time to keep myself in good physical shape, and I had no time to pursue outside interests, like writing. I was becoming an angry young man. I was simmering, but I was developing a deep and lingering sadness, and really questioning the purpose of life, and wondering how in the world I got myself in the position that I was in.

My life plan until that time was fairly simple: do my best, do what I was told, impress the right people, say the right things, get the right degrees, endorsements… and my life would be set. I would reap the rewards. Not only did the rewards lose their meaning, but in the micro-culture of large corporate law firms, this advice didn't always pan out. I saw many associates follow this model, give eight to ten of their best years, consistently working 70-80 hour weeks (sometimes more) only to be politely shown the door and denied partnership because they weren't the right "fit" for the firm. The idea of "fit" confused me, because some of the associates who were denied partnership were generally well liked. They had made the strategic connections yet when their number was called they were left out. So if my only driver was the rewards, and I took no intrinsic value in what I was doing, I was playing a risky game. Was I "fit"? How would I even know?

There was a hierarchy within the partnership. However, the hierarchy wasn't based on being the smartest, being the hardest worker, or being liked by the greatest number of people. Some of the highest paid, and most well known lawyers, were actually the least friendly; least liked generally, and didn't always have the top academic record. This confused me and this was clearly contrary to what I had previously thought. In many cases the lawyers who I most identified with, in terms of personality and educational background, were not the ones with the highest profiles, largest pay cheques and desirable lifestyles. They were often the ones putting in the long hard hours alongside the other toiling associates.

My Descent into Depression and My Decision to Re-educate

I would do my best to try to understand what the partners wanted, and give it to them, but I was frequently met with indifference at the best of times, and hostility at the worst. The game, that I once felt mastery over, was now taunting me, and it seemed like there was no end in sight. As soon as I conquered one element, it reset with an entirely new set of variables.

Also, my goals had become unclear. I didn't care about the rewards that they were offering. I didn't care about putting in more hours for more pay, and the work itself was not intrinsically rewarding. I had no compelling vision for the future that I wanted to create. I had always operated under the short-term assumption that once my objectives were met then the long term would clearly define itself. I discovered that this wasn't the case. Without a plan, I was on a road to nowhere, and chasing success just left me continually unsatisfied. Undergraduate quickly turned to law school, which morphed into a life that I found myself not wanting, not being intrinsically motivated by, and frequently wondering how I could get out of.

I would often wander the halls of the law firm, not to be seen (which was a funny habit of some insecure associates) but rather to observe. I wanted to see the partners. I wanted to determine for myself whether I actually desired what they had, and what they were—whether the goal of this silly game was compelling enough to continue. I wanted to know what the goal of this game even was? Was it a corner office? Was it a better suit, or faster car? Was it a bigger house? Was it my name in one of the industry publications? I didn't care about that stuff. More frightening was the question of whether I would ever actually enjoy what I was doing. All throughout school I had been motivated by money and prestige, but when I finally started to make money, and had enough of it to live a decent life, making more of it didn't motivate me, and the prestige felt hollow.

Most days I found myself in a paper prison. Surrounded in solitary confinement by contracts, agreements, and circulars, all of the documents that were supposed to be so important. I was in the heart of the high financial world, yet I felt so disconnected, alone and disempowered. My learning was always in a silo—a particular assignment on an isolated document from the partner of the day. I didn't feel like I was being groomed. I was caught in limbo, climbing a giant staircase to who knows where, and I didn't even care about the top.

It didn't take much until I knew in my heart that this was not the life that I desired. I didn't care about being a prestigious partner; I didn't even enjoy the law for the law's sake. But I didn't know where to go or what to do. I didn't know what the alternative was. I was terrified because I had spent so much time, and money, obtaining this career. If it was wrong then what was right? I felt that my entire life was completely unstable, and I questioned my mental stability. I suspected a transfer to another firm or legal environment would just yield the same results—and I had already been at two firms in two years. Some people already viewed that as flaky.

I also believed that I was held hostage because of my past. How could I change now? I had come so far. I had invested over 10 years of my adult life and well over one hundred thousand dollars in real costs and lost wages to get my education. How could I turn my back on this? What else would I do? How could I support my little family? What would my parents say? These questions were constantly on my mind as I lived half alive. It created massive anxiety and fear. I started to get panic attacks. I started to get emotional, scared and irrational. I would have waves of debilitating anxiety. Sometimes I couldn't get out of bed. On the best days I would wake up in a heavy mood, my head buzzing with the reality of having to do something I disliked but yet felt trapped in.

Carrying on the façade of interest became very difficult to maintain. I started to duck work. I started to lie. I started to be "busy" when the partners summoned me. I was strategic enough to find long-term projects that kept me occupied to avoid a rush of urgent time sensitive work. My personal dishonesty was unsettling. My subconscious screamed "hypocrite," but my tired soul wouldn't listen. I started leaving work during the middle of the day. I got real brave, even to the point of being careless. I would walk around downtown and observe people during the middle of the day. I would look into their faces. Prior to this I had always been in such a rush to get where I was going. My head was always down, my mind on the matters that were pressing. Now I walked slowly, head up, looking into the eyes of people around me.

Each day I would ride the train home after work. I would see the tired faces of my travelling companions. I would rarely see passion and excitement, except when a child was on board. I visualized life as a factory worker in the industrial era: devoid of excitement and passion. Each day was a hard day; having to do what was necessary for the day's pay. I would look around at all the passengers and wonder how much life had changed? Our living standards were much better, we were in nicer clothes, and we had the luxury of technology and safe working conditions, but I wasn't sure there was a difference in terms of our psychology. From a personal fulfillment perspective I felt nothing in what I was doing. I felt dead inside, I felt like an industrial factory worker in a suit, putting in my time for the day's pay. Was this the rest of my life? Was this all there was—trading time for a new suit or nicer car? That thought was tremendously painful.

I remember one day riding home on the train, reading *The Fountainhead* by Ayn Rand when the words of Howard Roark, justifying his choice to be an architect, seemed to jump off the page at me, "*You see, I have let's say, sixty years to live. Most of that time will be spent working. I've chosen the work I want to do. If I find no joy in it, then I'm only condemning myself to sixty years of torture.*" I was living opposite to this mindset, in a form of material driven, self-prescribed torture.

I wasn't Howard Roark. I was Peter Keating. I was the chameleon—constantly changing my personality to gain favor with others, to get ahead, but never feeling whole, succeeding on the outside, and dying within. Never feeling the intrinsic value of work, for the sake of work, not for the sake of rewards. I wondered if this would ever get better and if, or how, it could get worse. I rationalized, thinking that if I could just make more money, stick at it long enough then none of this would matter. I'd be ok. But deep down inside I knew that this was a lie. I knew that I would have to make a change in order to feel complete, and I wondered when I would summon the courage to change. I wondered if I even had that courage inside of me?

I had to find a solution quickly. My depression was real. My panic attacks frequent and increasingly painful. I was descending into a dark, dark place. If I didn't find a solution on my own I would need medical help. In the culture that I was raised in, "depression" was not acknowledged. We had a "suck it up and get back to work" mentality. So I felt ashamed to seek professional help, and I had no one to talk to. Also, I was terrible to be around. I was angry and quick to fight. I was also emotional and distant. I was distant to my wife and to my kids. All that I wanted to do was go to the gym and run. It was my escape, but like the treadmill that I was running on, I never seemed to go anywhere. I would wake up and be exactly where I was when I went to bed: sad, confused, anxious and depressed.

Nothing provided relief, but I had a seed of fight in me still. I wanted to figure out a way out of it, and I wanted to do it on my own. I wanted to use my mind to find a solution. I realized very quickly that in order to make an effective long-term change, I would have to re-educate myself. I would basically have to unlearn everything I knew about the world, completely restructure my decision making model, and start a new path, one that surely would be scary, but one that deep down inside I knew would lead to fulfillment—to empowerment.

Checkpoint:
Our Education and Our Empowerment

✓ Schools were not designed to develop the creative genius of individuals.

✓ Our schooling prepared us to take, and execute, instructions, it didn't teach us how to be fulfilled.

✓ Our schooling conditioned us to respect authority and to fear failure.

✓ In order to be fulfilled we need to continue our education, but outside of the classroom.

✓ In order to be empowered, we may need to make some difficult changes.

Chapter Two

The Process of Re-Education: Pursuing Flow and Mastery

Our World Is Not the World That Our Parents Were Raised In

The Internet has created an unprecedented opportunity for us to connect, form and build communities based on common interests and beliefs, and share things that we find valuable or meaningful. Never before in human history has there been a time where it was so easy to find exactly what we want instantaneously. Whether it is a product, a service, an idea, a song, a message, a relationship, a new job, a new religion, a vacation: everything that we could ever want or need can be found within a couple searches and clicks of the mouse.

The Industrial Revolution was replaced by the intellectual and connectivity revolution. With the Internet we are able to transact business across international borders, and penetrate geographic barriers that, because of costs, would have been inaccessible fifty years ago. Organic world of mouth marketing, the cornerstone of a successful business's marketing strategy, has been amplified by a million percent, as value propositions, ideas, products and services get shared through social media channels to create viral trends.

Many view these changes as disruptive. It is easier to just ignore them and pretend they aren't as powerful as they actually are. Some still see the Internet as a utility rather than a revolution. Others think it is just a fun little tool that allows us to send pictures to each other, watch videos, and buy stuff without having to leave our homes. It is this, but it is also so much more. Because of the Internet, our story, our message, and our products are being conveyed to the world, whether we like it or not. As Chris Anderson, Editor in Chief at *Wired* magazine and best-selling author of *The Long Tail,* notes *"Your brand is not what you say it is…It's what Google says it is."*[1]

The communities that are created on the Internet have real power. Politicians who generate social media momentum have a real advantage in an election; particularly with younger voters. Online communities also have a real influence on consumer spending patterns. Author Mitch Joel, in his book *Six Pixels of Separation*, detailed a number of studies to make this point:[2]

- Community users spend 54% more money than non-community users." (Ebay, 2006);

- Community users remain customers 50% longer than non-community users." (AT&T, 2002);

- Community users visit nine times more often than non-community users (McKinsey, 2000);

- 56% of online community members log in once a day or more." (USC-Annenberg School Center for the Digital Future, 2007); and

- 43% of Internet users who are members of online communities say that they 'feel as strongly' about their virtual communities as they do about their real world communities." (USC—Annenberg School Center for the Digital Future, 2006).

---

1   Joel, Mitch. *Six Pixels Of Separation: Everyone is Connected: Connect Your Business To Everyone.* New York: Business Plus, 2009. Print. 6.

2   Joel 68.

Since the World Is Different, Schooling Should be Different

As a result of the Internet, the rules that were rock solid generations ago don't apply as consistently anymore. However, some still cling to what they know, and many well intended parents, school counselors, youth leaders, and coaches give the same career advice that was given to them by their parents, before the Internet even existed: go out and get the most formal education that we can (despite the high real and opportunity costs) and herd into the job market. Take the best offer and stick with it for as long as possible.

The problem with this advice is that obtaining a traditional education will not necessarily provide the economic security that it may have provided in the past. The availability of virtually free information has made formal learning less valuable. Also, the ability to transact business and develop meaningful relationships is now nothing like it was thirty years ago because of the Internet. If we are fortunate enough to find economic security in the traditional method, there is no guarantee that we will actually enjoy working in what we do. Meanwhile, there are many examples of people, including myself, who were able to find fulfillment and economic success, outside of our chosen area of formal studies, and for some, even without a traditional economic pedigree.

How I Started to Re-educate Myself

My experience with formal education, and working for some of the most "prestigious" law firms taught me a clear, brutal, but critically important lesson: the systems, structures and rules that exist in the world are not designed with my "happiness" in mind. A factory education only made me smart in a sense that memorizing what an instructor wanted me to know made me smart, and only in a sense that doing what I was told, and doing that really well, made me smart. It wouldn't necessarily help me in those circumstances where I was left alone to think for myself. It wouldn't help me where I had to be brave and where I had to create. It wouldn't help me figure out how to add value to others.

It taught me how to be one of Taylor's factory workers, a good and obedient employee. I became well versed in how to take and execute instructions, and how not to ask questions. However, it didn't teach me anything about enjoying my life or finding engagement or happiness in my work. I wouldn't get that from a Professor or a formal course—these lessons I had to figure out on my own.

I realized that my multiple degrees and secure employment didn't bring me happiness and fulfillment because the actions that I was engaged in each day weren't aligned with my core interests and values. My actions and decisions were actually based on fear: fear of economic instability, fear of failure, fear of uncertainty and risk, and fear of criticism and social rejection.

I trusted that the system would just take care of it all—that all I had to do was play the game and do what I was told and I would be happy and fulfilled. I soon realized however, that by maintaining this mindset I had actually been a passive observer in my life. To be fulfilled, I couldn't be passive; I had to take an active role in thinking about what I actually wanted. I had to determine this with clarity. It wasn't enough to want a generalized sense of "economic security," "social acceptance" or "success." I had to seek a path of specific mastery, one where I was intentionally seeking something that was meaningful to me, independent of the thoughts or external rewards of society. I had to intentionally design my life and accept the path that resulted, risks, failure and all.

The Difficulties in Taking an "Intentional Life" Approach

Designing a life—it's much different than making a living. Unfortunately we often focus on the latter (as I did for many years). In our society, nothing sells quite like fear. It is impossible to watch the evening news without being completely inundated with the terrifying prospect that is our world. The economy always seems to be in a state of disrepair. We are constantly looking for a political savior to heal our problems and to deliver us from our woeful state. A secure job is always in short supply. The emotional premium we place on safety and security is dramatically enhanced by the focus that the media places on danger. It is impossible to consistently hear this message without at some point being influenced by what the talking heads are telling us.

Security, and fear of economic disruption, was the underlying motivation behind the advice of all the well-meaning people in my life who told me to pursue the academic programs that I pursued, and to take the initial jobs that I took. Such a tremendous premium was placed on economic security that it was nearly impossible for an impressionable young man like myself not to believe that getting as much formal schooling as possible, to make my life as free from risk as possible, was the best path. Very few people, during my formative years, encouraged me to pursue a path of fulfillment, even if this path was conventionally risky, difficult, painful or hard. As a result, when I made critical choices relating to my career I valued security over fulfillment. In fact, I hadn't even spent the time to clearly determine what I believed would make me fulfilled.

Stepping into the Void and the Risky World "Out There"

After I summoned the courage to leave the economic security, and emotional void of my job as a corporate associate at a large law firm I started my own law firm as a sole proprietor. This decision was the most logical transition for me to gain long-term clarity on what I wanted to do with my life. I would be able to alleviate the constant pressure of big firm billable hour quotas. I would start to feel the sense of autonomy and control associated with charting my own course. I knew that running my own law firm was not a long term plan, but it gave me a foray into the world of entrepreneurialism, and would allow me to adapt and seek clarity on what I wanted to make my life's work.

Even so, it was still a very scary venture. I described my feelings at the time to a close friend as "both terrified and ecstatic." I would seek to control my own fate. This prospect made me ecstatic. However, I did not have the luxury of a monthly pay cheque to rely on, and I had a mortgage and three kids. This prospect made me terrified. For the first time in my life I would have to create money by providing value to others. There was no "taking orders" and "doing my job." I had to figure out a way to bring in money. This was scary, but the fear didn't outweigh the pain of depression at my previous firm. So I went forward

I had many people in my life at the time, including lawyers at both previous firms try to dissuade me from making such a choice because of the "difficulty out there" and the security that I had where I was. I get a kick out of the concept of "out there." I'm not sure where "out there" actually is. But wherever it is, it is a scary place. I have since left the active practice of law, to pursue writing, speaking, consulting, and entrepreneurial ventures full time. This work brings me happiness, and it is work that I am committed to master, but I still continue to receive the same well-meaning advice whenever I pursue anything unconventional. A friend recently told me that she wished that she were as brave as me. I told her that bravery had nothing to do with it. The difference between us was simply that I understood the risks that exist on a traditional path, and I don't consider them to be greater than the path that I am on.

The Riskiness of the "Live To Retire" Model of Career Design

Making a living is the primary motivator for many of us when choosing what to study in school. It is the well-meaning intention of many parents who encourage a particular profession over another. It is the theme of the baby-boom generation: be safe, get a good education and a good job, make a good living, buy nice stuff, save and retire. Don't worry too much about day-to-day fulfillment; just think about all the golfing and travelling we will do when we are sixty (and have arthritis). This "live to retire" decision-making process has always struck me as illogical, and quite risky. Why spend our whole life doing something we dislike just so that we can make the path to death as "comfortable" as possible? And what happens if we die at 63? Our entire life is wasted because we didn't get to golf as much as we wanted? What happens if we don't even like golf?

When a parent has had a hard economic life, and particularly if that parent missed out on formal education, they are going to be supportive of the conventional path. Not because they have actual evidence that this is the correct path, but because they associate their lack of economic prosperity with a lack of formal education. Perception becomes reality. They view the world through their own economic hardship paradigm and they dearly want their children to avoid the same hardships that they had to endure. Their motivations are pure, and based on love. To them, the answer is simple, get a good formal education and any economic woes will be solved.

However, this association is not necessarily a definitive picture of reality. There are numerous, and well known, examples of people who attained economic prosperity without formal education. Much of industrial America was built on the work ethic of immigrants who arrived with hardly anything, other than dreams and an undeniable work ethic, and later earned economic prosperity. Even more telling is the fact that for many of us who have post-secondary degrees, we don't actually make a living doing the thing that we went to school for.

Learning is a wonderful thing. I am constantly, even obsessively, educating myself. I am, and continue to be a proponent of it, especially the continual learning that takes place outside of the walls of a conventional classroom. I love the Japanese concept of *Kaisen*, and I try to practice it in my life every single day. People who embrace continual education, and constant and never-ending improvement, as a fundamental component of their personality, have a distinct advantage over people who look to continually pacify themselves through entertainment or other distractions. However, it is a misleading, and potentially dangerous proposition to suggest that a formal degree alone will provide continual economic security and emotional fulfillment.

Schools are a product of industries. They are factories that pump out workers who can be slotted somewhere in the assembly line of life. We can obtain a skill set leading us to a profession—a doctor, a lawyer, a dentist, or an engineer. Alternatively we can learn some other skill (trade) that will allow for certainty of employment and certainty of income. My social network discouraged liberal arts and other "non-practical" programs because they couldn't equate into a direct monetary application. That is, they couldn't easily be parlayed into a job that would provide income stability and security.

I believe that many of us chose educational paths not because of the future fulfillment of what we would be doing, but because of the potential income security that our jobs would provide. So from the very beginning we are "living to retire." We are waiting to quit. Many of us weren't even aware of what we would be doing in our profession (in terms of the day to day activities) before we enrolled; this was clearly the case for me with law.

But it really doesn't matter, because there is a time slot in the great factory of life that needs to be filled and the more protection for the factory worker the better. The more golf we play when we are sixty, the better. I don't even like golf.

It's not this way with everyone. There are brave souls that have always forged their own paths. There are people that choose paths of fulfillment, despite the inherent associated risks. But I believe that these people are not the traditional majority. They are a brave and inspiring minority. Meanwhile the masses merge into the life of the metaphorical factory worker, piling into our cars like a herd and "heading to the factory of existence" each day when the morning bell sounds. Then at five or six, when the bell rings again, heading back home where we try to find fulfillment in the fleeting hours. Yet we rarely have the energy to fully embrace these hours. So for many, life is a day-in, day-out engagement, the same process, a factory worker's life, trusting security, and fearing the harsh realities of the world, doing it all so that we can "quit" and "retire" someday. This model is depressing and uninspiring.

If a choice presents itself between security and fulfillment we are encouraged to take security. There is nothing wrong with this underlying motivation, and it is very common for us to value security as a foundational virtue. However, there is no guarantee that obtaining a traditional education, and entering into the traditional job market will actually lead to economic security. There is no guarantee that the "live to retire" model will actually allow us to "live to retire." If this is the case, then we have to live with the very real prospect that we could do something we don't enjoy our entire life, and still not have economic security. What a terribly depressing thought. If we don't get financial security we at least should be fulfilled.

Even if we are able to successfully navigate the traditional educational path (and its real associated costs) and effectively integrate into the job market, there is also a real risk that we will end up exactly where I did—thirty years old, eight years of post-secondary education under my belt, hating the position that I found myself in, feeling trapped, and stuck, and growing increasingly depressed, and knowing that the only way out was scary and involved massive change, change that would have been much easier as a twenty year old, unmarried adult without kids.

The Discovery That I Was Not Alone,
Others Were Living in Quiet Desperation

I used to think that I was alone—that somehow I had just missed the memo of life. After I left law, I created the habit, which I still continue to this day of writing very honest, real and heartfelt posts about my career on my personal blog, www.ryanclements.com. As I started to figure out my core values, and seek out entrepreneurial, consulting and writing engagements I started to feel a newfound passion for life, so I wrote about it.

The more honest I was, the more traffic that my blog seemed to generate. Then what happened next was the inspiration for this book. People started to reach out to me. People started to email me, and share with me their stories, many of which were very similar to mine. This was when it sunk home that I really wasn't alone. I realized that there were actually many individuals who were just like me. People who had successfully navigated the factory education system and still failed to find fulfillment, and who were now in careers they felt offered little by way of long-term emotional engagement.

Many of the people who sought me out told me that when they read my blog, and my experiences, they thought that I was telling their life story. I started to make connections with new people who were equally caught in this trap. I realized that there were many like me, and I wanted to help them. I wanted to give them hope and contribute to them by telling my story and helping them to see that they were not stuck, they had options, if they were able to overcome their fears and align their actions and goals with what they truly valued.

Money and Status Are Weak Motivators,
We Want Happiness and Meaning

We are searching for meaning in our lives. It is no longer sufficient for us to have a "secure nine to five" if we feel that our employment offers little by way of personal meaning for us. Daniel Pink in his wonderful book *Drive, The Surprising Truth About What Motivates Us*[3] provides strong support to

---

3   Pink, Daniel. *Drive, The Surprising Truth About What Motivates Us.* New York: Riverhead Books, 2011. Print.

the suggestion that traditional motivational tools are not working anymore and that now employers must adapt to keep quality people engaged and productive.

Carrot and stick motivation, or what Pink labels *"Motivation 2.0,"* although serving some purposes, fails to work as it should, because it is unreliable and assumes that we rationally maximize wealth at all times. The reality, as Pink aptly identifies, is that all people are irrational, some of the time. We make errors in judgment because of a number of psychological factors.

Pink suggests that the primary reason that carrot and stick motivation fails to properly work is that it actually ends up extinguishing the intrinsic motivation for performing the activity that people are being rewarded to perform (or punished if they fail to perform). This is exactly what happened to me. I was completely driven by external rewards (the grades, the degrees, the social status, the economically secure and prestigious job) to the point where once I thought I had sufficiently received enough of my "prize" (with emphasis on "enough") I lost all internal motivation to continue on the path. As a result, the rewards based motivation, so prevalent at law firms— the money bonuses for grueling billable hour targets, and the "hope" of one day becoming a partner—made it virtually intolerable for me. I just didn't care about these rewards. Pink continues,

> Rewards can perform a weird sort of behavioral alchemy: They transform an interesting task into a drudge. They can turn play into work. And by diminishing intrinsic motivation, they can send performance, creativity, and even upstanding behavior toppling like dominoes.[4]

This is also exactly what happened to me as an undergraduate student when I had that formative experience with my macroeconomics Professor. A part of my desire to learn, for the sake of learning, died, and I've had to work really hard since then to get it back. My paradigm shifted so that I saw my education purely as a results-based game. A game with a carrot at the end—an external reward for whatever I had to put up with, even if that was an arrogant and disinterested Professor. School turned my intellectual

---

4   Pink 35.

curiosity into drudgery because it now wasn't about learning—it was about finding out the "right answer"—it became about getting a reward.

Pink cites many examples of behavioral studies that lend evidence to his position, including the well-known studies of Mark Lepper and David Green on intrinsic and extrinsic motivation of preschoolers drawing in their spare time.[5] The results of the study are clear and resounding—there is a very real risk of destroying internal motivation by providing external rewards for the successful completion of a task.[6] This may not happen initially, in fact in the short term, there is often an increase in the performance of the task. However, in the long run there is a real risk that intrinsic motivation completely evaporates. Pink notes,

> Try to encourage a kid to learn math by paying her for each workbook page she completes—and she'll almost certainly become more diligent in the short term and lose interest in math in the long term. Take an industrial designer who loves his work and try to get him to do better by making his pay contingent on a hit product—and he'll almost certainly work like a maniac in the short term, but become less interested in his job in the long term.[7]

Unfortunately, our factory system of education is completely based on external rewards—the carrot (a degree and the prospect of secure employment) if we are successful and a stick (an uncertain future) if we aren't. Further, many employers still use this type of motivation to reward employees: higher pay and bonuses for performance (the carrot) and the prospect of losing our job if we don't perform (the stick). So what happens to many of us is that the hope of external rewards and recognition makes us more diligent in the short run (during our schooling and the early years in our career) but after a period of time our intrinsic motivation for doing our job fades, we become disinterested, and in many cases (as was the case for me) the prospect of continuing similar employment for decades is discouraging, and depressing.

5   See Greene, David, and Mark Lepper. *The Hidden Costs of Rewards.* Hillsdale, N.J.: L. Eribaum Associates, 1978. Print.

6   See Kohn, Alfie. *Punished By Rewards: The Trouble With Gold Stars, Incentive Plans, A's, Praise and Other Bribes.* Boston: Houghton Mifflin Co., 1999. Print. See also Reeve, Jonmarshall. *Understanding Motivation and Emotion.* 4th ed. Hoboken, N.J.: John Wiley & Sons, 2005. Print. 143.

7   Pink 37.

Rewards Aren't the Answer, Intrinsic Motivation Is, Here Is How We Develop It

There is evidence to suggest that if we are able to maintain our intrinsic motivation into our professional careers we are more likely to be successful than if we stick with our unfulfilling jobs solely because of the hope of continual rewards (like secure retirement and a continually stable pay cheque). [8] If this is the case, an interesting paradox is presented. It would seem that the people who are the least motivated by the rewards of their performance are the same people who are able to generate rewards because of their performance. More importantly, the people who are very motivated by the rewards of their performance (those who stay in unsatisfying jobs to maintain stable pay) are often the ones less likely to generate the rewards they seek. So it would seem to suggest then that maintaining intrinsic motivation is a critical element to performance.

So how do we do this? How do we maintain intrinsic motivation? How do we create for ourselves a career that is both personally fulfilling and economically viable? How do we navigate our world, and the great emphasis it places on external rewards, without losing intrinsic motivation? Is it possible to have both personal fulfillment and economic security? I believe that it is; however, the path is not a "conventional" one, neither is it a collective one. I believe the path is an individual one. It involves first finding out what we uniquely value—what things are uniquely "us"? What things are meaningful to our core?

Our core values serve as a compass to help us navigate our life's purpose. Once we have determined our core values and life's purpose then we must commit to that path regardless of the risk, and independent of any reward. We must seek the path, not because of what we are going to receive from that path, but rather because the path is intrinsically motivating in and of itself. We commit to a path of becoming the best that we are capable of becoming in relation to our life's purpose. When we do this, we are no longer driven by the external rewards of society and we are more likely to find engagement, fulfillment, and I believe long-term economic security.

---

8   See Getzels , Jacob and Mihaly Csikszentmihalyi. *The Creative Vision: A Longitudinal Study of Problem-Finding in Art.* New York: Wiley, 1976. Print.

Checkpoint:
Rewards Are Not the Answer, Intrinsic Motivation Is

✓ Carrot and Stick motivation, while very prevalent in our schools, doesn't foster long-term positive career alignment.

✓ Money and status only work in the short run, they later lead to discontent.

✓ The only form of motivation that works in the long run is intrinsic motivation, we must actually enjoy what we are doing.

✓ Those motivated by "the work," not "the reward," tend to create the best work.

✓ Intrinsic motivation occurs when our unique core values align with our goals.

Understanding What We Uniquely Value, and Avoiding the Universal Value Trap

To have economic security in today's world we must be able to provide something that is meaningful and valuable to other people. To tap into the unique value that we can provide, we must first determine what it is that we value as individuals. What core values motivate us most to action? It is important when assessing our core values that the "universal value trap" doesn't catch us. The "universal value trap" is based on the observation that there are certain values that are universal, in a sense that pretty much everyone values them to some extent.

If the values that we identify as our core values are "universal values" then we will have a difficult time coming up with a life purpose that will provide a continual source of intrinsic motivation and personal satisfaction. Common "universal" values are economic security and social acceptance (love). When

I discovered this I realized that just about all of the "career" driven decisions that I had made in the past, such as going to law school, and pursuing a career with a large law firm, were motivated by the underlying "universal" values of economic security and social acceptance.

I was seeking my social group's approval and admiration, and becoming a successful attorney would place me in their highest esteem. My social reference group also suggested that the path that I was pursuing was the safest (economically speaking) so I had the added reinforcement of this "universal" value being met. When I was in law school the motivation of having the admiration of my professors and the notoriety of my fellow students made the big firm option most appealing. Also, I was very aware of the earning discrepancy between big firm lawyers and those who pursued alternative career paths.

Making decisions based on "universal" values did not bring me to a place of happiness. Also, once I had achieved a reasonable level of economic security and social acceptance in my career, I noticed that my intrinsic motivation started to dissipate very quickly. I didn't have the extra "push" that was needed to make things great, master the subject matter, or endure pain or discomfort. I was driven by my need to be "acknowledged" as successful, and to make a decent living in the process. By graduating from law school, and getting a high paying job, I achieved both of these goals. So once my goals were met I was left feeling hollow, and not having the desire to go the extra mile anymore—primarily because the only thing that was being offered in terms of incentives by the law firms were more of what I already had (money and prestige).

After I left law, one of the first things that I did was analyze myself, and determine what values were unique to me. I wanted to gain clarity and certainty on the things that I valued. I saw my life as a clean slate, a way to rebuild where I didn't need to play the game that had brought me unhappiness. I knew that if I could tap into my own unique voice then I would have the best chance of creating a proposition to the world that was worthwhile. The first step in determining my core values was to ask myself this question, "At what times in my life had I been the most happy, content and fulfilled."

The honest answer to this question was not what we would ordinarily think. It was not the vacations or moments of entertainment or indulgence that I had experienced up until that point in my life. It was also not the recognition, social esteem, accomplishments or "successes" either. Having made a decent income for a number of years prior to my departure from law I had begun to experience the "nicer things" of the world—good vacations, nice cars, nice clothes. These things did not come to mind when I honestly answered this self-directed question. Here is what I came up with (not in any particular order):

1. I was most fulfilled when I felt absolute freedom to pursue any path I wanted. When I was unconstrained by social pressure or feelings of expectation to act in a certain way I felt most at peace;

2. I was most fulfilled when I was contributing in a real way to others—adding real value to their lives, helping them grow and find happiness, without any expectation of reward or compensation;

3. I was most fulfilled when I was communicating with others, through writing or public speaking;

4. I was most fulfilled when I felt that my life had an element of adventure or risk in it. The times of uncertainty in my life were actually some of the most fulfilling for me;

5. I was most fulfilled when I was engaged in the act of creation, taking a thought and giving it life through my actions;

6. I was most fulfilled when I was spending time with my family;

7. I was most fulfilled when I was exercising my body and living as healthy as possible;

8. I was most fulfilled when I was learning new things, reading new books and ideas and continually educating myself; and

9. I was most fulfilled when I was challenging myself—pursing self-directed goals, of my own choosing, that caused me to give the very best that was inside of me. I was happiest when I was engaged in self-directed difficult work.

After I comprised this list I could see so clearly why I was unhappy in law. Not only were most of my core values not being met, but also in some cases my career was actively fighting against them. Law had placed many of my most important values in direct opposition to the universal values of security and social acceptance.

The most revealing example was found in my value of freedom. Lawyers bill by the hour, time equates to money, and there are no means of being rewarded for adding value through efficiency or creativity (at least at the firms I worked at); therefore, I never truly felt free. If I wanted to increase my financial stability (universal value of security) then I needed to spend more time at the firm on billable matters. If I wanted to gain the respect of the firm partners (universal value of social acceptance) I needed to spend more time attending law firm social events and networking engagements. I had to make myself known as a "team player," someone who would forgo my own personal plans for the needs of the firm. All of these were encroachments on my freedom.

I had a conversation with a senior partner at my firm when it was time for my associate review. I had not received the same level of bonus as some of the other associates so I asked the partner whether my work was the same quality. The partner answered that it was, in fact he said that it was better than many. So I audaciously asked him why I wasn't being compensated for it. He said that the other lawyers had billed more hours. I told him that I intentionally tried to work as fast and efficiently as possible so that I could get home to my family. Only after doing this value analysis did I fully realize that my unique values of freedom and family were being full-court pressed by the universal value of security (which at the time was being met by my job as a lawyer).

The assault on my time was ever present by the prison bracelet that commonly identified itself as a Blackberry. The unspoken mandate of being "available" at all times, whenever necessary, was suffocating to me, and a real contributor to a sense of great despair in my life. I recall one time getting home from a long, hard, workweek. It was Friday night and I returned home at about 7 pm. I had no established work responsibilities over the weekend so I took the bold step of literally turning my nemesis off. I spent some much needed time with my children and wife and left it off for the remainder of the night. When I turned it back on Saturday, later in the morning, it immediately lit up with multiple messages from a firm partner requiring my urgent action on a hostile takeover bid. Even before I could read the messages, the red flashing light on the blackberry triggered a Pavlovian rush of anxiety throughout my body. I knew exactly what the messages would say before I even read them.

Not only did my time in big law encroach my freedom and alienate me from my family, it also created a disempowering environment for my other unique values. I rarely had the flexibility to maintain a consistent exercise regime. My diet was frequently met with fast food and other high caloric, and convenient, options as a result of working through lunch and dinners at the office. There was very little sense of adventure in wading through stacks of contracts or drafting long information circulars, and it was impossible to pursue writing and public speaking opportunities at the time, other than engagements in areas that the firm wished to have a profile in (which areas didn't interest me). Further, I didn't feel that I had any "self-directed" challenging goals, and I wasn't creating anything. Sure meeting billable hour quotas was challenging, but these were firm mandated goals, not goals that I uniquely embraced, or even chose for that matter.

If I had performed a unique value analysis ten years earlier, and if I would have had the maturity and foresight to not overweigh the universal values of security and social acceptance, I would have made a different career decision. I believe that I would have arrived at the place that I am now, but much earlier. After performing this analysis I knew that I needed to spend the rest of my life in these forums: entrepreneurship, business development, writing and public speaking. I knew this because these arenas facilitated most my core values, and were all intrinsically rewarding.

Right now, my wife and I run a small business from home that is engaging, exciting and provides a real value to others. I also pursue independent consulting, writing and public speaking projects. I significantly utilize the Internet to facilitate all of these ventures. All of these activities are aligned with my core values of freedom, adventure, contribution, creation, communication, and education. Because I am my own boss, and can determine my own hours, I also have the ability to pursue physical fitness, family and spiritual goals as well. All of this contributes to a much greater sense of purpose, well-being and fulfillment.

The path that I chose in my life is conventionally much riskier, in the eyes of some people (much more on the concept of risk to come in later chapters); however, since my core values are being met I am tapping into my own unique voice. Also, since the path is one that I have independently chosen, I desire to master the subject matter. This desire for mastery makes the intrinsic value of performing my work greater than the external rewards of success. At a minimum, I am not driven by the external rewards, I truly love what I do, for the sake of doing it, independent of what I can "obtain" from doing it. As a result, I want to do it for as long as possible. Also, I believe myself to be on a much safer long-term path, one that more than anything else, will help to provide economic security and personal fulfillment, but most importantly, one that will provide emotional engagement since I am embracing the struggle. I am pursuing mastery of the subject matter.

Re-educating Myself:
Learning to Pursue Mastery, Not External Rewards

Mastery is an intensely difficult, but extremely powerful pursuit. Robert Greene in his book, *Mastery*[9], defines mastery as a personalized sensation, "*a feeling that we have a greater command of reality, other people, and ourselves.*"[10] He notes that for people who master their fields, this feeling becomes a part of their everyday life, "*their way of seeing the world.*" The path to mastery involves very hard work, and the ability to sustain ourselves through mundane tasks until we are proficient. It requires consistent and sustained education, control of our emotions and fears, and great patience. Many will discard a life of mastery, deciding instead that the path is reserved for a select few who, because of genius, social privilege, innate talent, or just dumb luck, are able to live exceptional lives. Like Greene however, I believe differently. He notes:

> Over the centuries, people have placed a wall around such mastery. They have called it genius and have thought of it as inaccessible. They have made it seem as if it were as elusive as magic. But that wall is imaginary. This is the real secret: the brain that we possess is the work of six million years of development, and more than anything else, this evolution of the brain was designed to lead us to mastery, the latent power within us all."[11]

---

9   Greene, Robert. *Mastery*. New York: Penguin Group, 2012. Print.

10 Greene 2.

11 Greene 5.

Green articulates three phases in the pursuit of mastery. The first phase, or *"Apprenticeship Phase,"* is where *"we stand on the outside of our field, learning as much as we can of the basic elements and rules."*[12] Since we only understand our field partially we are limited in the powers that we have, and the abilities that we have to influence and progress. The second phase Greene describes as the *"Creative-Active"* phase. In this phase we immerse ourselves in the field and through continual repetition and practice we begin to understand what we do on a deeper level. Greene notes, *"we see inside of the machinery, how things connect with one another, and thus gain a more comprehensive understanding of the subject."*[13] Once this takes place we are able to get creative and experiment in the subject matter. The final phase is the phase of Mastery. Concerning this phase Greene states,

> In the third phase, our degree of knowledge, experience, and focus is so deep that we can now see the whole picture with complete clarity. We have access to the heart of life—to human nature and natural phenomena. That is why the artwork of the Masters touches us to the core; the artist has captured something of the essence of reality. That is why the brilliant scientist can uncover a new law of physics, and the inventor or entrepreneur can hit upon something no one else has imagined.[14]

The steps to mastery are difficult, and require long-term sacrifice. Results are not immediately visible. Therefore, in our "quick-fix" society there are very few people who will actually sustain the path to mastery. Instead, many will accept a path to "security" in the form of material comfort, and the "live to retire model," merely making the path to death more comfortable, not the path of life more fulfilling.

As Greene notes, many people *"become slaves to time—as it passes, we grow weaker, less capable, trapped in some dead end career."*[15] This is exactly the state that I found myself in only three years into my career as a lawyer. When I read the following excerpt from Greene's book I felt like he was talking specifically about me.

---

12   Greene 3.

13   Greene 3.

14   Greene 3.

15   Greene 9.

Conforming to social norms, you will listen more to others than to your own voice. You may choose a career path based on what peers and parents tell you, or on what seems lucrative. If you lose contact with this inner calling, you can have some success in life, but eventually your lack of true desire catches up with you. Your work becomes mechanical. You come to live for leisure and immediate pleasures. In this way you become increasingly passive, and never move past the first phase. You may grow frustrated and depressed, never realizing that the source of it is your alienation from your own creative potential.[16]

I did not listen to my own voice when I entered the legal profession. I saw it as secure and lucrative. I saw it as prestigious, and a status position in society, an external reward for my educational sacrifice and abilities. It became increasingly mechanical as my actual career started. I never saw stage two of mastery—where I had a comprehensive knowledge of the subject matter, because I just didn't care. I found a way to migrate into practice areas that were primarily driven by law clerks and paralegals. Each day I would "manage," I would "oversee." My benchmark of success became not getting sued for negligence and making enough money to vacation as often as possible (and thus escape) and drive the nicest car I could. This passive engagement in life, this focus on leisure and immediate pleasure, this desire for escape, absolutely was a contributing factor to depression.

Greene notes two keys that are necessary in order to pursue a path of mastery, both of which I have embraced. First, we have to believe that our pursuit of mastery is critical—it is absolutely necessary in our life. Also we must believe that this pursuit is a positive one. For me it became critical because I could no longer accept a life that I was sleepwalking through. I had so much more to give. I had to step into my fear, and decide to pursue my passions to mastery. The pain of what I was doing, the emotional void that I felt each day, the depression that was ensuing was so real, and it was so painful, that I had to make a change. The second key that Greene notes is that we must have an internal locus of control. We must actually believe that we have the power to shape our own minds and our experience through our actions. We must actually convince ourselves that we are responsible for what we see.

---

16 Greene 14.

Locus of control is a theory in psychology that refers to the degree to which an individual believes that they can control the events in their life. Those with a high internal locus of control believe that they can shape the events in their life. They believe that the results they achieve are derived from the actions that they take. This type of person will not make excuses if they don't get what they want when they want it, rather they will look inward instead and ask empowering questions such as "how can I do better?" "what do I need to change?" and "what are others doing that I can incorporate into my life to make it better?"

Those with a high external locus of control believe that they are victims in the world. They believe that they have very little control over their lives or the events that happen to them. They may give their best towards achieving a goal, but if they don't get the goal then they look to direct the blame at something or someone other than themself. They constantly blame others and external circumstances, and play the victim card, if their life doesn't go exactly as they want, exactly when they want it to.

People with a high internal locus of control are more likely to seek to influence others in a positive way. We are generally not one or the other; we exhibit both external and internal tendencies from time to time. I realized that for a large part of my life I had an external locus of control. I didn't realize that I had power to direct my own reality. I felt that other things controlled me. But what I eventually realized was that all of the things that "controlled" me were actually just barriers that were created in my own mind. I started to do the following and I discovered that my locus of control shifted to internal:

- I started to focus my attention on making small daily goals and completing them. This gave me momentum and I began to realize that I had the ability, internally, to make things happen with respect to my ultimate desire;

- I started to surround myself with other people who were internal locus of control, and who were pursuing their unique dreams and goals, not just accepting what had been given to them in life. This influenced how I thought. I realized that my worldview was just my worldview. Other people didn't share it; and

- I cut out media that was causing me to be externally focused. News on television was a big one. Every time I watched the news I would doubt my ability to succeed as an entrepreneur or establish a writing career. Once I stopped the habit of consuming daily television my attitude and outlook changed.

When we align our decisions and actions with our core values, pursue an individualized path with passion, one that we believe that we can control, one that is intrinsically motivating regardless of external rewards, and commit to that path to the point of mastery; we are then able to create value in the world. In the chapters that will follow I will highlight many examples of individuals, organizations and companies that have used new media marketing and the Internet to do this. Also, I will discuss how their boldness is impacting the world for the better. In addition, I will present the framework for how ordinary people, like us, can pursue a similar course.

Checkpoint: The Keys to Mastery

✓ We have to believe that our pursuit of mastery is critical—it is absolutely necessary in our life, and it is a positive endeavor.

✓ Mastery requires hard work, dedication and sacrifice.

✓ We must first accept being an apprentice and learn all that we can from a master.

✓ When we immerse ourselves in our field, through continual repetition and practice we begin to understand what we do on a deeper level.

✓ At a level of mastery, we can provide significant value to the world, and we also receive rich compensation, not just with money, but also more importantly with internal satisfaction.

Re-educating Myself: Learning to Pursue Flow and Intrinsically Motivating Goals

When we are on the path of mastery, we are pursuing things that are personally meaningful regardless of external rewards, and our path is aligned with our core values, we are likely to also experience a mental state of "flow." The concept of flow, as first articulated by Dr. Mihály Csíkszentmihályi[17], former head of the Psychology department at the University of Chicago, is a state of optimal experience, or the set of conditions when a human being is most fulfilled. Optimal experience is not the result of wealth, perceived significance, or any other form of social status. Rather, optimal experience occurs when we achieve a state of completely focused motivation, or single-minded immersion, where our mind and body are stretched to their absolute limits in a voluntary effort to achieve a difficult and worthwhile goal.

Dr. Csíkszentmihályi suggests ten factors indicative of a state of flow:

1. Clear goals, where the expectations and rules are discernible, the goals are attainable and align appropriately with one's skill set and abilities, and the challenge level and skill level are appropriately high;

2. A high degree of concentration on a limited field of attention;

3. A loss of the feeling of self-consciousness (otherwise described as the merging of action and awareness);

4. A distorted sense of time in that our subjective experience of time is altered (time seems to "stand still");

5. Direct and immediate feedback with respect to the goal such that successes and failures in the course of our activity are apparent, so that behavior can be adjusted as needed;

6. An appropriate balance between ability level and challenge in that the activity cannot be too easy, nor can it be too difficult;

7. A sense of personal control over the situation or activity;

8. The activity is intrinsically rewarding, so there is effortless action;

---

17 Csikszentmihalyi, Mihaly. *Flow: The Psychology Of Optimal Experience 1ˢᵗ ed.* New York: Harper & Row, 1990. Print.

9. A lack of awareness of bodily needs, to the extent that we can reach a point of great hunger or fatigue without realizing it; and

10. An absorption into the activity with the result of a narrowing of the focus of awareness down to the activity itself.

It is easy to see how determining our core values and pursuing mastery and intrinsically rewarding activities channels flow. Our goals are clear and compelling, and fear of social pressure doesn't motivate them. As a result, we experience a sense of control, or at least a sense of participation in the determination of our outcome. We have an intrinsic sense that we, and no one else, are the driving force before behind our life. We are constantly learning, refining our skills, and adapting our abilities to the challenges that present themselves. As a result we are becoming more complex as human beings. Also, because the pursuit is something that is internally valuable we are easily able to concentrate on the task at hand.

Most importantly, because the actions involved in the pursuit of our goals are related to our core values it is much easier to find intrinsic enjoyment in the pursuit itself. As a result, we are not focused only on the rewards of our actions. This makes the process of losing ourselves in the engagement natural and time stands still. It triggers "effortless action." Paradoxically, it is when this type of behavior is consistently applied over time that great results manifest. When we place our focus on the base needs of security and social acceptance and design our careers around these values we rarely are able to tap into the energy, internal drive, creativity and passion resultant in obtaining a state of flow.

Unfortunately, many of us don't ever tap into flow. We don't feel the great internal rewards that come when in a flow state. Work for many is only about the reward, which is why it is called "work." It is about "doing what is necessary" to get the pay cheque. Our society places great value on materialism, to the point that we will consider ourselves failures, relatively speaking, if we don't make as much money as our peers. This belief is a big mistake. We are better off emotionally and psychologically making less money and channeling flow, than making more money and being externally driven. When flow is channeled repeatedly in a career great results become manifest, and money becomes an echo of the creation of value.

Case Study in Mastery and Flow: Helio Gracie and Brazilian Jiu-Jitsu

Perhaps one of the best examples of the power of value-centered purpose, when combined with the relentless pursuit of mastery and flow, is that of the Gracie Family[18] and the way that they have spread their art, Brazilian Jiu-Jitsu (BJJ), throughout the world. The origins of BJJ are well known. In the early 1900s Mitsuyo Maeda was sent overseas by Kano Jigoro, the founder of the martial art of Judo, to demonstrate the art and spread it's influence. Maeda, one of Jigoro's top students, arrived in Brazil in 1914.

A young and impressionable Carlos Gracie watched a demonstration by Maeda, and decided he wanted to learn the art. Gracie began the process of study under Maeda, and would later teach what he learned to his brothers. His youngest brother, Hélio, was a sick and frail boy, and was under doctor's recommendations to not train, given the risks that the full contact sport posed to his weak body. For years young Hélio would sit on the sides, watching his brothers train, studying the various holds and locks, informing his mind before his body had a chance to engage. Carlos by this time had been giving paid lessons in Judo to local businessmen and others interested in self-defense.

On one fateful day, a student arrived for his scheduled lesson, with Carlos being late and not present. Seizing the opportunity, Hélio offered to begin the class for the student. When Carlos arrived the student was so impressed with young Hélio's teaching methods that he asked Carlos if he could continue to learn under him. Carlos agreed and Hélio's teaching career began. Judo involved many throws and other techniques that relied on physical strength in order to implement. Because Hélio was such a small man he had to adapt the traditional Judo holds and locks to maximize principles of leverage, and minimize the necessity of physical superiority in order to exact dominance. His frailty created a necessity—he had to adapt in ways that could be utilized without physical strength. As a result, BJJ became very popular, because it presented the possibility for a smaller individual to defend and even defeat much larger adversaries.

---

18 Jeffrey, Douglas. "Helio Gracie on Brazilian Jujutsu" *Black Belt.* March 1999: 24. Print. See also Associated Press. "Helio Gracie, Promoter of Jiu-Jitsu, Dies at 95" *New York Times*, 29 January 2009: <http://www.nytimes.com/2009/01/30/sports/othersports/30gracie.html?_r=1&> Web. 12 June 2013.

Hélio's trial and error adaptations not only transformed Judo into an entirely different art, the art of Gracie or Brazilian Jiu-Jitsu, but it also propelled him into the spotlight as the art's most famous practitioner. Hélio became so convinced of the superiority of his art, as compared to traditional fighting styles, that he famously challenged any and all comers in public exhibition bouts. Even as a 5'9", 130 pound man, Hélio was able to defeat or at least fight to a draw much more physically gifted and stronger men, including champions in other fighting styles from around the world. Hélio became a well-known sports figure in Brazil in the 1930s as his adapted art began to receive public notice.

Jiu-Jitsu became much more than a physical exercise to the Gracie family. It became an art, a lifestyle, a philosophy; some would even say a religion. Spreading the art became the family's purpose and the mastery of their art of fighting was continual. Carlos and Hélio formed the Gracie Academy where BJJ would be taught to all those who would come. The most important academy that they would create however, to further the interest of their sport, was the academy within their own home. Carlos, who had twenty-one children, and Hélio, who had nine children, purchased land and developed the "Gracie Compound," a large property in Teresopolis, Brazil with a Hotel style house and it's own water tower.[19] The mission of the Gracie compound: to teach the Gracie children Jiu-Jitsu.

Ultimate Fighting Championship co-creator Rorion Gracie, Hélio's eldest son, was one of the children who were taught the art at the hands of the master. In an interview for a biopic of Hélio on the *Biography Channel,* Rorion provides a humorous description of what it was like "growing up Gracie":

> When people would drive past the house in Teresopolis, they would see all the kimonos neatly hanging outside, looking like straitjackets. You would look at the grassy area at the center of the house, and on the canvas in the grassy area, there were people training. It looked like a mental asylum...crazy people...thirty-five children grappling with each other.[20]

19 The Fight Works Podcast. "Gracie Jiu-Jitsu Compound" <http://thefightworkspodcast.com/2012/06/17/gracie-jiu-jitsu-compound/> Podcast. 12 June 2013.

20 The Fight Works Podcast. "Gracie Jiu-Jitsu Compound" <http://thefightworkspodcast.com/2012/06/17/gracie-jiu-jitsu-compound/> Podcast. 12 June 2013. See also Biography Channel. "Helio Gracie Documentary" <http://www.youtube.com/watch?v=jo6sG1UqQAs> Web Archive. 12 June 2013.

As part of the training regime, Carlos and Hélio also created a special diet (the "Gracie Diet") designed to maximize health and nutrition by focusing on food combining for optimal health. These "little grapplers" grew into some of the most famous names in the now thriving world of mixed martial arts including original Ultimate Fighting Championship Winner Royce Gracie, and his undefeated older brother, Japanese Vale Tudo Champion Rickson, and it is these men (Carlos' and Hélio's) sons who have completely altered the world of competitive martial arts forever through their teaching and influence. Anyone who is familiar with mixed martial arts is familiar with the Gracie family and BJJ. All of this came about because a family had laser like focus on a life purpose and a complete dedication to mastery.

Winning competitions, making money, and achieving fame and status were never goals for the Gracie family, although these results have surely followed them over the years as the popularity of their art has flourished throughout the world. Gracie Barras, or teaching academies, can now be found globally. The family's focus, as first established by Carlos and Hélio, has always been on sharing their art with the world, and proving to the world that what they created was a superior martial art form. The path that they pursued was not one based on external rewards, but one that was based on absolute and complete mastery of a subject matter.

Hélio Gracie died at the age of ninety-five having lived a full life dedicated to mastery of his chosen life's purpose. Rumor has it that he was still training in Jiu-Jitsu, and instructing students, only ten days before he died. There is no question that he lived a life that engaged flow. He didn't chase external rewards, but rather sought, even until his very last days to master, in essence to perfect, his purpose. This is a philosophy worth emulating. Each of us can have that too, if we are willing to do what it takes. The path is simple. We must determine what we value and what is intrinsically rewarding; we must then align our actions and goals so that they correspond to these values. External rewards (money, security, prestige) cannot be our sole motivating driver, but rather we must embrace a life that is dedicated to the mastery of a unique, and self-contained, purpose. An empowered life embodies this unique purpose.

Checkpoint: For Empowerment
We Must Pursue Mastery and Flow

✓ It is important to figure out what we uniquely value, and avoid the "Universal Value Trap" of financial security and love.

✓ Pursuing mastery of what we uniquely value, rather than external rewards, leads to lifelong fulfillment.

✓ Flow is an optimal human state where we are stretched to our limits in a voluntary attempt to achieve an intrinsically worthwhile goal.

✓ When we pursue what we uniquely value we are likely to experience a flow state, continually develop in personal complexity, and never grow discouraged or bored in our pursuits.

Chapter Three

Breaking Free by Understanding Fear and Risk

The Pull of a Creative and Compelling Life Vision

Once we have established what we uniquely value, the next step is to create in our minds a clear picture of what exactly it is that we want. What makes us come alive? What is an area that we would be willing to master, to spend the hard time learning, and growing, and struggling, and even failing at times, so that we could be in a position to truly add value to others? What is an area that we could create, and sustain, a unique value proposition to the world? At this point it is necessary to use our minds to create a clear and compelling vision for our life. Many people never fully engage in this creative exercise. As a result, they never experiment with the creative process of asking the question "what would my life look like in the best case scenario?"

If we engage in this process it is very common to censor our real desires, or substitute what we really want for material acquisition or status. If something seems "unconventional," or "unrealistic" then sometimes we won't include it in the creative vision. As a result, we'll end up focusing on "making a living" rather than "designing a life." We'll set impotent goals because we fear. It is also our fear that will lead us to made decisions based on obtaining security and social acceptance. In order to create unique value it is necessary to become comfortable with risk. This process is much easier when we realize that every path is risky. Unfortunately, we often live in a personal story in our head that overemphasizes the risks in pursing a creative vision and downplays the risks of a conventional path.

Also, being dreamers, and even worse, having the audacity to actually believe in our ability to achieve our dreams puts us at odds with the social majority. Loved ones and family will try, for our sake, to bring us down to earth because they don't want us to get our hopes up, and see us experience pain if those hopes come crashing down. Others, particularly those who have never had the courage to pursue their true desires, will also criticize us or look for flaws or try to find fault in our plans or our ability to achieve them.

This is why allowing the universal values of security and social acceptance to guide us is so dangerous. We don't want to let ourselves down and feel that "we are not enough." We don't want to feel insignificant or inadequate if we fail. We don't want to be ostracized from our social circle. We don't want to validate our doubters. We are often terrified of not making ends meat. As a result, we are very reluctant to engage in any exercise where we "dream" for more, especially if that dream involves risk of losing what we have.

A clear and compelling vision for exactly what we want out of our life, when aligned with our core values, has a tremendous pulling influence on us. Dreams are a projection of the life we wish to lead. Therefore, when we allow them to pull us, our dreams unleash a creative force that can overpower all obstacles hindering the attainment of our objectives. To harness this power a dream must be vivid, clear and compelling. A fuzzy and vague picture of what we want out of life has very little pulling power. The more clearly we define our dream, the better we describe it, the stronger it will pull us.

A Creative Vision Eliminates the Need for Willpower

This entire process takes place without having to resort to willpower. Willpower is what is needed when there is an external stimulus and an externally controlled reward. Willpower is what we have to use to "convince" ourselves to keep going, and the most readily accessible tools of persuasion are visualizing the pleasure of the carrot, or realizing the pain of the stick. Many people use willpower to get out of bed in the morning, and go to their unfulfilling jobs, when they would much rather stay cozy and warm, or watch TV, or do something "fun" instead. They know however if they don't get out of bed then they may lose their job (stick), which will cause pain. They also know that if they can just get through the day (and the month) then they will get their pay cheque (carrot), which will allow them to buy stuff that is pleasurable.

The problem is that the months turn to years and the years turn to an entire life—an entire life where willpower is necessary. Willpower isn't necessary when we are pursuing a creative vision properly aligned with the things that we uniquely value and are intrinsically motivating. In this case effort is easy and flow is abundant. There is a pull effect. When a creative vision is present we find ourselves staying up late into the night working on making our ideas a reality—thinking, dreaming, and working. We tap into flow and time seems to stand still. We wake up with ideas to implement, no time to waste, and we rarely find ourselves "stalling," or searching for the "entertainment opiates" in the form of TV or random internet browsing.

So why is it that we don't often pursue career paths that align our core values with our day-to-day goals and actions? Why is it that we just go through the factory education system, find a "job" that pays the bills and then spend the rest of our time pursuing financial goals, engaging in hobbies, and other pursuits, until we can "retire"—that is quit from active life. Retirement is basically a "vacation" until death. This is such a depressing vision of life. As a society, why do we spend more time planning our death, and making the path to death as comfortable as possible, rather than planning our life, and actually attempting to carry out a life that is meaningful?

In many cases the answer is simply fear. A life that is personally meaningful can be risky to pursue. This path is often not as "secure" as a conventional path. We may dream of being a writer, or an artist, or starting our own company to add value to the world, but we think that these are very risky or unrealistic ventures, so we come to the "logical" conclusion that life would be better if we just lowered our standards a little and instead found enjoyment in hobbies, entertainment, and perhaps relationships. Besides that is the smart thing to do. That is the practical thing to do. So we get into a field or career that will provide a stable income, job security and consistency. In many cases however this job does not provide fulfillment, and that eventually leads to emotional problems down the road.

Fear Sells, Fear Works:
We Must Learn to Manage Fear or It Will Manage Us

Fear is an ever-present part of our world. We can trace its roots to evolution, and our fears of being the next meal, or having our livelihood destroyed by the next marauding invader. As conscious analytical animals, we are constantly aware of the many threats to our existence and stability. Therefore we learn to survive, and fear and protect against things that can threaten our safety. Fear is conditioned in us from the time that we are kids. In grade school, we learn to fear giving the wrong answer, fear the bad marks, fear not getting into the right program or right school, and fear taking a position that is contrary to our teacher. As we grow older we fear losing our jobs, and not being able to make a good living and support our family. We fear not saving enough for retirement and being alone and helpless. We fear not being able to help our kids with university and schooling. We fear, we fear, we fear.

We are all painfully aware of how effectively fear sells. The media constantly uses it, every single day, to influence and drive attention. We cannot watch a news program without learning of some disaster, crime, concern, or pending calamity around the corner. Companies use it in their marketing campaigns to scare consumers into believing that something bad will happen to us if we don't purchase a certain product. The avoidance, or removal, of potential pain or discomfort is then a very motivating factor for us to open our wallet and part with our hard earned money.

Special interest groups use fear to promote their agendas. Politicians use it to get elected and promise that they will "take away our problems" and save us from the terrible risks that are always looming around the corner. Attack ads litter the television and the Internet during campaign season, making us concerned about the "hidden agendas" that a candidate may have, or the "terrible consequences" to all of us if a particular individual is elected. Such consequences rarely, if ever, materialize. The terrorists, the economic instability, the melting of the icebergs—everywhere we look, there is a wolf around the corner, and we need someone to save us.

Despite being the most technologically proficient species it is remarkable how often we make decisions that are influenced by fear. I believe that it is possible to get to the point where fear doesn't pervade all of our decisions, however we were socially and biologically conditioned to abhor risk and cling to safety, and as a result, a deconditioning must take place to come to empowering terms with the prospects that induce fear, and learn to act in spite of them.

Learning to Manage Fear: Survival-Empowerment Inventory

This method is perhaps one of the simplest, and most practical, I have learned in dealing with fear. I call it the *survival-empowerment technique*. First, ask yourself this question: "what is the worst thing that can possibly happen?" Often the worst thing that we can think of has basically no chance of manifesting itself. For example, very few people die or lose loved ones by changing careers. Usually the worst-case scenario is simply failure. Failure will then trigger a chain of events that are possible, for example having to go back to our old employer and ask for our old job back. If the job isn't available (which it's often not) then it may be necessary to get a different job, take a step down in income, dip into some savings, or sell the boat. Usually that is the absolutely worst-case scenario. In all likelihood the worst case scenario won't happen, but we'll run with it for a moment.

The next step is to ask this follow up question: "can I handle it?" Our response may surprise us. At first we may think that a career setback or a "visible failure" where we become the subject of criticism would be the worst thing in our life, but when we really internalize this prospect we realize that we have the inner fortitude to handle it. Not only do we have the ability to handle it, but the more we look at it from this angle the more we realize how silly this little fear was in the first place, and we begin to feel foolish that we allowed ourselves to spend so much time worrying over something that clearly we had the emotional ability to handle.

This analysis has a dramatic empowering effect on us, because we actually realize our own inner strength instead of being hypnotized by the pervading culture of fear that surrounds us. We realize that we are actually brave. We realize that we have the inner strength to deal with a failure or setback. If we experience a setback or a disappointment we will just look for an alternate route to our destination. It is like a feedback mechanism, and it is characteristic of being in a state of flow. We become much more likely at this point to identify the values that are most important to us and then make changes, even if those changes are scary, difficult or challenging, because those changes are necessary to get us closer to our goal.

Now we have momentum in dealing with our fear. Now we are starting to feel brave, even powerful. So then we take the analysis one step further. We ask ourselves this powerful question: what is the best possible thing that could happen? It is necessary at this step to use the neglected muscle of our imagination to visualize the fulfillment of our best-case scenario. Even better is to experience the visualization by asking ourselves these follow-up questions: "how would I feel if this took place" and "what does this mean to me?" This exercise induces a powerful emotional state and excites us to take action. We start to experience again the pull power of a crystal clear and compelling objective.

Checkpoint: For Empowerment
Survival Empowerment Inventory Questions

1. What is the worst thing that can possibly happen?

2. Can I handle it?

3. What is the best possible thing that can happen?

   How would I feel if this took place?

   What does this mean to me? To my family?

Learning to Manage Fear:
Visualizing Past Victories or Learning Experiences

Other ways to come to terms with disempowering fear is to visualize a situation in our life where we successfully conquered fear or learned a new skill. If we can recall an experience vividly then we can induce an emotional state similar to how we felt in the original instance. Once this emotional state is induced then we simply remind ourselves that this new challenge is the same as the previous one that we successfully navigated. Just like the previous experience, we may need to learn a new skill set in order to be successful in our new endeavor.

We must never forget that fear is the companion to growth. We cannot grow unless we learn. We can only learn when we encounter, for the first time, something that was previously unfamiliar, and then navigate the unfamiliar setting so that it becomes familiar. The correct path is not to try to eliminate fear entirely. Fear cannot be eliminated. Fear is an emotional response giving a signal that we are in unfamiliar territory; it is actually a good thing. The correct path is to simply take action to navigate the unfamiliar territory, and make the unfamiliar territory familiar. When this happens fear will dissipate because we have mental and emotional references telling us that we have been here before, and we can handle it.

We must educate ourselves as to the rules of this new territory. The problem is never the fear itself; it is how we hold the fear. It is what the fear does to us. Does it cause us to act, or does it paralyze us from action? If we hold fear as inhibitive then we experience feelings of helplessness, depression and paralysis. When we hold fear as simply an emotional signal to action then we experience education, energy and empowering choices.

Learning to Manage Fear:
Fulfillment Waits for Us on the Other Side of Fear

In the past year I've learned some amazing lessons about fear by studying Brazilian Jiu-Jitsu, because Jiu-Jitsu forces me to confront a primal fear: the fear of pain and literal physical confrontation. Jiu-Jitsu is a submission art, where skills are learned and refined through actual fighting. I cannot "only drill" or take instructions, I have to grapple, I have to fight, I have to learn what it feels like to be submitted before I can learn the skills necessary to submit. This involves temporary pain. There is no way around it.

Here is the first lesson that I've learned about fear from doing Jiu-Jitsu: fear is triggered every time an unfamiliar situation comes up; however, when I experience the situation (thereby changing the unfamiliar to familiar) the fear dissipates. If that situation comes up again I'm no longer scared. Fear will return however if a new, unfamiliar, situation presents itself.

On my first class it was scary to even show up (because I didn't know what to expect). That soon went away by just showing up lots. Then, it was scary when I first "experienced" the various submissions applied on me for the first time. That fear went away after "feeling" those experiences. Then, when I started rolling with other white belts, it was scary at first. But that fear went away after rolling for a little while. Then it became scary when I first started rolling with colored belts, but after rolling with several of them, that fear went away as well.

This leads me to the second lesson I've learned about fear from doing Jiu-jitsu: when I actually experience what I am scared of, I come out of the experience feeling really good about myself. I have a sense of internal fulfillment that is unlike almost anything I've previously felt. I believe that fulfillment is on the other side of fear because when we walk through our fears we become more complex as individuals. We are forced to grow, and with this growth comes confidence and happiness. When we become more complex, as individuals, we are internally satisfied. Our confidence grows, and so does our happiness. So when I experience fear (which I know I will as I encounter new situations) I know that it is just a signal, letting me know that there is an opportunity at my door for growth, and ultimately for more happiness and fulfillment.

It Is More Than Just Fear: We Don't Understand Risk Very Well

It goes much deeper than just fear. Fear, and social conditioning, is a simple answer. There are also flaws in the way that we conceptualize and comprehend the principle of risk. When we become aware of the various psychological tendencies that we have as human beings, and how these tendencies are further impacted by social dynamics, we can see that risk is often more a function of perception than reality. It is also a product of conditioning. Social influence, and societal norms and conventions can have a tremendous effect on the subjective lens that we see the world through. What we find when we study the psychology of risk is that not only are we "risk selective," but also at times we experience "risk confusion" when it comes to making decisions that lead to long term fulfillment.

Why We Don't Understand Risk Principle #1: Confirmation Bias

The first way we are often impaired in our ability to realistically interpret risk is through the principle of "confirmation bias." All people, at various times, have experienced this principle: we view the world through a subjective lens that acts to give confirmatory support to our pre-determined beliefs. Everyone has beliefs about the "way things are" or the "way things are supposed to be." These beliefs are formed by multiple influences: our social conditioning, our environment, our education, our worldview, the experiences we have had, the experiences that those close to us have had, and many other factors. Once a belief is formed, all subsequent information that is received, potentially impacting the original belief, is either embraced (if it confirms the original belief) or viewed critically, and ultimately discounted or disregarded (if it contradicts or raises a doubt with respect to the original belief).

It doesn't even matter if the only basis for holding a belief is simply that those around us, those we most frequently associate with, also hold this belief. Once a belief is formed, information is constantly screened in a biased way to ensure that our beliefs are not jeopardized. The most obvious example of this is in orthodox religions where people become argumentative when their beliefs are questioned. Instead of responding rationally to evidence, we flatly ignore it, or get hostile towards it. Confirmation bias is rampant in orthodox religions. This screening process distorts reality and causes us to discount, or flat out deny, the existence of facts or information that counteracts, or fully disproves, our beliefs.

Take for example someone who has formed a belief that traditional education is the only path to economic security. That person will see the world through a very particular lens. They will give more weight in their minds to the examples of entrepreneurs that fail and struggle and have to return to more traditional jobs (and lose their lifestyle and toys in the process). They will sustain their particular worldview by selectively embracing the information that is available. They won't see the many examples of entrepreneurs who succeed, create jobs, and a live a life of fulfillment by adding value. These will be seen as anomalies in their mind. They will also significantly discount the number of individuals who are very discontent in life, despite successfully navigating the factory educational system. Their worldview is sustained by clouding the facts, by having a confirming bias in all of the information that is presented to them.

One could argue—well aren't I doing the same thing right now? If my belief is that the traditional educational system isn't designed for the fulfillment of its participants won't I view the world through a biased lens? The answer is of course. Confirmation bias works both ways, for everyone. That is why my analysis of risk selection, and confusion, is not based on confirmation bias alone. There are many other factors all of which accumulate to an interpretation of our world that may not be based in reality when it comes to making career decisions.

Why We Don't Understand Risk Principle #2: Group Polarization

The next principle is what is often described in psychological literature as "group polarization." It's basic premise is that when people of a similar mindset or belief habituate, their beliefs (even if those beliefs are not founded in reality, are irrational, or in the worst case are dangerous or destructive) will not only crystalize but will also grow more extreme. A very real example of this concept is in dangerous religious cult behavior such as the David Koresh led Branch Davidians in Waco Texas, or the mass suicides of the People's Temple, led by Jim Jones in Guyana in the 1970s.

Dan Gardner in his book, *Risk* describes the theory of group polarization as the phenomenon that takes place when people who share beliefs get together in groups. He suggests that when this happens, people will believe, to an even greater extent, that their beliefs are correct, and they may even become more extreme in those beliefs.[1]

The community I grew up in was an intersection of farming, and natural resources based small businesses. There were a smaller number of educated professionals, usually occupying the customary positions of lawyer, dentist, family physician or chiropractor. Where I grew up many career options were not endorsed or discussed. In fact, they were unheard of—literally. The Internet did not yet exist, and many modern career options relating to business, communications, public relations, non-profit and education, literally weren't known by many of the good people in the town I grew up in, including the teachers.

As a result, to a promising young student like myself, the encouraged path was that of a professional. The only frame of reference for entrepreneurship was smaller businesses, many of which struggled. The group (my community) collectively supported the belief that there were few options available in terms of a career: I could be a farmer, a teacher, start a business, or go to school and get some type of professional education. If I didn't do any of these then I'd either work in sales, or work as an employee for someone else. The safest of all career routes was that of a professional. The principle of group polarization not only supported this belief but also strengthened it.

Another example of group polarization that I directly experienced was the insular culture present in large law firms. Many of the individuals who populate these firms believe that they are part of the intellectual elite in the world, and in many cases, objectively this is true, these firms are fully of exceptionally intelligent people. Many of them carry forward their intellectual confidence one step further—into a belief that they have arrived at a very prestigious place in society. The firm, the partnership, the money they make, each of these are symbols of their achievement. The status, and importance of their position in society is enhanced by group polarization.

Big firm lawyers spend time with other big firm lawyers. There are quarterly magazines and publications specifically tailored to the big firm law culture (which magazines I now find quite humorous). In these publications, merger and acquisition "deal highlights" are described like adventure stories

---

1   Gardner, Dan. *Risk: The Science and Politics of Fear.* London: Virgin Books, 2009. Print.

or sports conquests. There are galas and awards nights honoring the top lawyers under a certain age—always determined by other lawyers by the way—and oddly enough the galas honoring these lawyers are almost exclusively attended by lawyers and their spouses (who are often lawyers).

Unfortunately these beliefs grow extreme within the group. So much that new lawyers, fresh faced out of law school, are almost indoctrinated by it. Wanting to fit in we model the beliefs of the partners—beliefs that have grown extreme because of group polarization. I now humorously, and remorsefully, recall the time that I came back to my farming town, while I was working at a large firm, and talking to someone about my law career. I remember almost a sense of intellectual distain because the person that I was talking to asked for advice on a small civil matter. Didn't he know where I worked? Didn't he know the big business we were doing? Obviously, if he knew anything, he should know that our firm doesn't handle that kind of stuff, I thought to myself. Those files are for the guys who didn't ace law school! I'm now embarrassed by how I once literally thought. But there are many who still think this way.

I remember, when the big law firms were recruiting me, that there seemed to be a caste undertone—there were "tiers" of law firms, and I didn't want to end up at the lower tier. Even some of my Professors fell prey to this, encouraging me to only go to the biggest, and "best" firms, not encouraging me to consider what I actually wanted to do with my life, or what I wanted to do on a day-to-day basis. Image was very important, more important than fulfillment.

I feel very bad to admit that this was how I once thought. I believed, like many other lawyers at the big firm that I was intellectually better than others because of my acceptance into their world. I bought into the beliefs that were made extreme by group polarization at the firm. I believed I was part of an intellectual elite. I believed I had status in life by virtue of my firm and my association with these people. I started to react to it. I started to talk and dress like them. It wasn't me. I believe it was a major contributor to my unhappiness at the time.

I remember distinctly the first crack in this foundational belief, and my first insight that my worldview was being clouded by the polarizing influence of the group that I was a part of. I was on a big merger deal and we were working hard hours, constant weekends, late nights—big bills for the law firm, but a big headache for the lawyers. I remember meeting one of the proprietors of the acquiring company at a meeting. He was a young guy, not too much older than me. I inquired what his education was. He didn't have any; rather he had built his company through risk taking, hard work and innovation.

In the course of our conversation it became evident how much he enjoyed his business, and the lifestyle that it afforded him. I remember on my way home on the train, after another late night drafting an information circular (the act of which I took very little interest in) thinking: if I'm so smart, If I went to school for so long, then how come I'm spending so much time doing something I don't like? If I'm so lucky to have this job, then why don't I embrace it? If this is such a status position, then what is the status? Why am I working constant sixty-hour weeks helping to build someone else's dream? Where is the status in that? Then I realized that perhaps I wasn't that smart. Perhaps I had accepted the belief that I was smart because of the polarizing influence of my group.

Why We Don't Understand Risk Principle #3: Representativeness and Our Consistent Irrationality

It was once widely accepted that we were rational decision makers. That is, we would always evaluate the available evidence, and in so doing make a decision as to which way we should act in a given situation to advance our rational self-interest. In other words, we engage in constant "cost-benefit analysis." If the cost of acting in a certain way outweighs the benefits of that action, then we will choose not to take a certain action. For many years, this rational self-interest theory dominated economic thought, and was also the basis for behavior modifying legislation (such as criminal law). If criminal deterrence was a goal, a legislator had to just increase the punishments that would apply to a particular crime to dissuade the criminal act.

The discoveries of future Nobel laureate Herbert Simon in 1957 caused a disruption in the unequivocal acceptance of rational self-interest theory. Simon, with his term "bounded rationality," hypothesized we are indeed rational; however, there are limits to our rationality.[2] That is, in certain circumstances we all make similar mistakes. Therefore a simple analysis based on costs and benefits did not completely illustrate how we would interpret information when making decisions.

In the 1970s, psychologists Daniel Kahneman and Amos Tversky, sought to determine in what situations we acted "consistently irrational," despite the availability of information that would motivate us to act otherwise. Their first publication on the subject, a 1974 paper published in the academic journal *Science* entitled, "Judgment Under Uncertainty: Heuristics and Biases" provided significant insights into what determined our sporadic, yet homogenous, habits of irrationality.[3] This paper was later expanded into a book of the same title, published in 1982, and since publication has had an important impact on our understanding of how we calculate, interpret and analyze risk.

The traditional cost-benefit rational self-interest model is based on certainty and clarity in determining costs and benefits. In an uncertain world (a world which is the norm, not the exception) we are forced to make decisions with uncertain costs and benefits. Also, the probability of cost, and the probability of benefit, is uncertain. Therefore our "rationality" is bounded by the concept of certainty. In an uncertain world we are prone to act in a manner, which ultimately isn't in our rational self-interest. Kahneman and Tversky sought to determine whether there were any "heuristics," or experience-based techniques for problem solving, learning, and discovery, that would influence our decision-making ability in the face of uncertainty.

In their paper Kahneman and Tversky revealed three heuristics, problem solving rules that can often impair our ability to rationally interpret an uncertain proposition. The first rule is called "representativeness." This rule is used to judge the probability that an object or event (A) will belong to a certain class or process (B). Simple ways to understand this rule is that when judging whether object A belongs to class B we will associate what is "typical" or "representative" of the class. A "typical" winter day in northern

---

2   See Simon, Herbert. *Models of Bounded Rationality: Behavioral Economics and Business Organization Vol. 2.* London: The MIT Press, 1983. Print.

3   See Kahneman, Daniel and Amon Tversky. "Judgment Under Uncertainty: Heuristics and Biases" *Science* 185:4157 (1974). 1124-1131. Print.

Canada is cold and snowing; therefore when judging the probability that it is cold and snowing on a winter day in Northern Canada, without any objective evidence, we will subjectively interpret the probability to be high. We give a high subjective probability because the event (being cold and snowy) is typical of the class (northern Canada in the winter).

Typical associations work in most cases. We can make a reasonably reliable quick judgment of the probability of a given event in relation to a particular class. Besides, it just "feels" right. It sits well with our "gut." However, the rule can go wrong when our view of what is "typical" doesn't match with the objective reality of a given situation. For example, Joe is involved in numerous social and public interest engagements. He campaigns for, and supports, his local "green party" candidate. He spent a summer in Africa as an undergraduate student building an orphanage. He sits on the board of a non-profit that raises money and awareness to help children involved in the illegal sex trade. Without any other information, what would be Joe's "most likely" occupation? A staffer for a left-wing politician, a research academic at a non-profit or NGO, a plumber, a farmer, or an analyst at a hedge fund?

Many people would automatically assume one of the first three options, not one of the last three, especially not the analyst at the hedge fund. Why is this? It is because working at one of the first three jobs (a class) would be "typical" of a person who shared Joe's interests and engagements (an object). What if in fact Joe was an analyst at a hedge fund, it is a possibility. We have no evidence, other than what is "typical," to suggest that Joe would be more likely to work at one of the first three jobs. We bring subject interpretation to our analysis based on representativeness—based on what we think is typical in a given set of circumstances.

Also, this rule is completely contingent on our interpretation of what is "typical." What if our analysis of what is "typical" is completely based on a subjective interpretation or some form of confirmation bias? What if we have no rational basis to form our interpretation of what is typical? Therefore, we make two subjective interpretations in any decision involving uncertainty, the sum of which leads to acting in ways that are not always in our own best interest. First, we subjectively interpret what is "typical" in a given situation, and then we use this interpretation to subjectively interpret whether our typical situation fits into a given class. We come up with a conclusion that is not only completely irrational but also not in our self-interest, but we go forward anyway because it "feels right."

Let me paint of picture to highlight how this heuristic can sabotage the career decision-making process. I know many people who are very wealthy, content, fulfilled and engaged having carved out a career in sales. Take young Robert—he may have the skill set, natural aptitude and ability to succeed tremendously in sales. More importantly, his core values may be freedom, communication, and social engagement, and he intrinsically likes talking to people: all core values that would align with sales-based careers. However young Robert has a "typical" association of salespeople that isn't based in reality—it is based on his subjective perception and his socialization. He believes that successful sales people are pushy and annoying. He also believes that they are not professionally educated, and that they had to go into sales because they had no other options.

When he is making career decisions he may apply the representativeness heuristic and predict that the probability of him succeeding in sales is low because it is "typical" (in his mind) that salespeople who belong to a certain class (successful) have certain characteristics (pushy, annoying and uneducated). He will think that the probability of his success, and happiness, is low because he isn't "typical" (especially given his interest in education). So he doesn't pursue the path, even though this path could turn out to be tremendously rewarding, engaging and personally fulfilling. Instead he pursues law and is miserable. His analysis was subjectively flawed because of the representativeness heuristic.

Why We Don't Understand Risk Principle #4: The Example Rule

The next rule than Kahneman and Tversky outline is commonly referred to as the "example rule." This rules suggests that in an uncertain situation, the subjective probability that a particular outcome will occur is influenced by the nature, and ease of recollection, of the instances or scenarios that the subject can recall. In other words, something will seem more likely to occur (in our mind) if we can easily recall instances of it occurring under similar settings. Kahneman and Tversky specifically call this heuristic the "availability heuristic." Author Dan Gardner describes this phenomenon as follows:

> This experiment has been repeated in many different forms and the results are always the same. The more easily people are able to think of examples of something, the more common they judge that thing to be.[4]

A perfect illustration of the "example rule" in a career decision making setting is the behavior of many lawyers who say that they would like to operate a business, yet never really embrace the challenge (other than passive engagement as an investor, corporate secretary, or board member). Corporate lawyers are professional risk assessors. However, they have no way of determining potential risk with a degree of probability (as we live in an uncertain world). Yet they can see a myriad of "possible" risks better than the average person (since they have been trained, and paid very well, to do so over a number of years). So consider a lawyer who may be very discontent in their current job. They may have friends who are entrepreneurs and deep down inside they may dream themselves of being a real entrepreneur—stopping the law practice all together and jumping in with both feet into a full time business venture.

The "example rule" reveals that the ease, and speed, at which lawyers are able to think of examples of ways that a business could go wrong, the more likely they will judge the probability of their own failure to be. This judgment isn't based in reality; it is based on the "example rule." I know lawyers who continue discontent at their job for many years, while full time business opportunities continually pass them by. Each opportunity is deemed too risky. They deem it too risky not because it necessarily is too risky, but because they are able to come up with many more ways in their head that it could fail than the average person. That is why sometimes (particularly for entrepreneurs wanting to start up a new venture) "ignorance is bliss."

An important distinction with respect to this rule is that it is not necessarily the nature of the examples of how the business could fail that the lawyer thinks of, or the number of examples. The real issue is how quickly, and the ease at which, the examples come to mind. This premise is supported by

---

4   Gardner 55.

studies by psychologists Alexander Rothman and Norbert Schwartz.[5] As a result, experience as a "business" lawyer doesn't necessarily prepare one to be a better entrepreneur. I could rationally argue that it makes me much more susceptible to the example rule, and thereby a worse entrepreneur, because I will not move quickly to seize opportunities. I will see a myriad of potential problems so quickly that I will likely hesitate or deliberate instead of jumping in with both feet.

When we combine this rule with the media's constant stream of negative and fear inducing noise, as well as the confirmation bias that many of us have with respect to traditional education and entrepreneurship, we can see clearly why many of us herd into traditional "jobs" rather than even try our hand at owning or running a business for ourselves. At the same time, the example of stability and comfort, in not dreaming, in just doing what we are told, and accepting our pay cheque quickly comes to mind. Objective reality may dictate that a "typical job" will result in, or continue to provide, serious discontent and discouragement (as it did for me) but the "example rule" acts as a real psychological barrier for people to actually change.

Why We Don't Understand Risk Principle #5: The Anchor Rule

The final rule that Kahneman and Tversky put forward is the "anchoring heuristic," commonly known as the "anchor rule." This rule suggests that any available statistic that we can recall, when considering the probability of risk, will serve as an anchor for us. In other words, if we are uncertain about a situation, or the probability that something will occur, we will search for the most recent number that we can remember being told relating to the context. After we have determined this, our logic will attempt to adjust this number downward, but in most cases we end up going back to close to the anchor number in our interpretation, even if the anchor is completely wrong. The fact that we had previously heard a number relating to the context, and more importantly, the fact that we can quickly recall it, has a tremendous effect on our psychology and how we interpret the riskiness of a given decision.

---

5   Gardner 55.

Psychologists Brian Wansink, Robert Kent and Stephen Hoch carried out a great illustration of this rule in a test on consumer purchasing preferences in grocery stores.[6] The test was to see how consumers would change their purchasing preference given variable signage. When a sign limiting purchases to 12 each, was present, the majority of customers purchased 4-10 cans of soup, and not a single shopper only purchased a single can. However, when the sign was removed, almost half of the customers only bought 1-2 cans. In this case 12 served as an anchor, resulting in customers buying more cans than they normally would without a sign. Marketers are very aware of this heuristic, and unfortunately use it to manipulate the buying preferences of customers.

Anchoring of another form is commonly seen in political debates. Figures are given as supposed "facts" and numbers are thrown out left and right by politicians. The numbers may have a slight basis in reality, but their basis is from a particular study, that includes certain set variables that may cause the figure to be inaccurate in the context (and in many cases the whole study itself is contested by the opposing party). However, the numbers are stated as definitive and when interpreted, and later recalled by observers, can serve as an anchor, impacting their judgment relating to the context in the future. In fact, a partisan observer will often use the exact same number in their personal communications relating to the issue without ever "fact-checking" to see if their party talking-head was actually quoting a correct statistic. When we are aware of this rule, and the way that politicians and others repeatedly manipulate numbers in the media, a political debate can take on a humorous undertone. Unreliable statistics have become part of who we are as a society.

An example of how the anchoring rule can distort career decision-making is the statistics that are often used to describe the failure rates of new businesses. I have seen many derivations of the same statistic, something to the effect that 9 in 10 businesses fail within the first year of their operation. However, when this statistic is quoted it is rare that there is any disclosure as to where the statistic came from, how it was generated, what businesses it dealt with, and where the study took place? Was it for part-time business

6   Gardner 42.

ventures? Was it full-time owners? Did it include home-based businesses, Internet businesses, and non-traditional ventures? What was the sample size? How was the data generated? When we apply all these questions we realize that this statistic is very unreliable. However, the use of the statistic has an impact on us when thinking about leaving our secure job to be an entrepreneur. We will anchor our perception of reality with the statistic that we recall and even if we adjust down, we end up close to the actual statistic that we believe to be true. This will add to our fear of the prospect of being an entrepreneur.

Our Social Nature Impacts Our Ability to Assess Risk

Another set of psychological phenomena that impacts our assessment of risk are the many tests that have confirmed our "social" nature, and the very real fact that what others think, and the decisions and choices that they make, matter deeply to us. There is evidence to suggest that not only does social influence impact our behavior, but it can influence us to such an extent that we will discount our own perceptions, even if those perceptions are correct, to follow the influence of the group, even if the group is wrong. Dan Gardner, in his book *Risk*, highlights this point by describing a now famous experiment by researcher Soloman Asch,

> In one of psychology's most famous experiments, Asch had people sit together in groups and answer questions that supposedly tested visual perception. Only one person was the actual subject of the experiment, however. All the others were instructed, in the later stages, to give answers that were clearly wrong. In total, the group gave incorrect answers 12 times. Three-quarters of Asch's test subjects abandoned their own judgment and went with the group at least once. Overall, people conformed to an obviously false group consensus one-third of the time. We are social animals and what others think matters deeply to us. The group's opinion isn't everything; we can buck the trend. But even when the other people are strangers, even when we are anonymous, even when dissenting will cost us nothing, we want to agree with the group.[7]

There are many reasons why we look for group support and confirmation. The evolutionary advantages of working in groups are obvious when

---

7   Gardner 119.

we consider the harsh circumstances of life thousands of years ago and the physical disadvantages we had compared to other animal species. Our ability to reason allowed us to pool our individual intelligences and form a collective mind, an intellectual synergy, that when coupled with collective physical effort, would result in continual technological progress, starting with simple physical structures and continuing on to what we see today—advancements in science, computers, telecommunications, architecture, construction, just about anything we can think of, to a degree that would have been incomprehensible only centuries ago.

So it seems that we are hardwired to follow the herd. It is in our biological nature (for the protection of the species), since the group offers the greatest level of support and protection. It is also a logical premise since the intellectual ability of one person is limited to what that person knows, or what they can learn, and no one person can learn all things, nor do they have the time or ability to implement their knowledge. As a society we look for the advice of "experts" on subjects that are not widely known in order to make decisions. However, what is more important than the advice of the expert is whether our trusted "group" to which we belong (our family, community, church group, political party, friends, etc.) also believes in the "expert's" message.

Most political hot button issues will have "expert" studies to support both sides of the ideological spectrum. This can be a confusing proposition for us to navigate. This is where the powerful principles of confirmation bias and group polarization kick in. If our reference group has a belief, which belief we also embrace, then the "expert's report" that contradicts our and our group's belief will be harshly scrutinized, and likely disregarded, and the report that supports the belief will be embraced.

Perhaps the most amazing example of this observation is with respect to global warming. On this subject there exists many scientific studies. Both political ideologies (right and left) use confirmation bias to flat out deny the existence of global warming on the one had, or discount, mock, and deny the existence of studies challenging its origin on the other. Therefore, an expert's report to confirm a belief is not nearly as important as the reference group's influence, and the fact that an individual has also accepted the belief as true.

So when it comes to career decision-making it is obvious why we generally trust the belief that successfully navigating the factory system of education will equip us with a meaningful and engaging career. We have accepted this belief for decades; therefore, confirmation bias will absolutely be present with respect to any information that may present evidence to the contrary. I suspect that confirmation bias is even present with people who are reading this book. It is a tremendously controversial position to suggest that a "traditional" education is not necessary to find fulfillment and economic security, and that given the Internet, with the exception of entering a "regulated" profession; we don't need to pay high priced tuition to gain all the knowledge necessary for success. Asch and Crutchfield's work suggests that even if we believe this, we are unlikely to admit it.

However, there exists evidence to the contrary. There exists many, many examples of personally fulfilled and economically secure people who either aren't working in their field of study, dropped out of post-secondary education to pursue a unique passion, or never attended at all. I'm not advocating for the elimination of the institutions of higher learning, I am just saying that assuming that the "system" will set us up for fulfillment is a dangerous, and false assumption. Further, assuming that the absence of traditional education will sentence us to a life of meaningless hardship and physical labor, is a dangerous, and false assumption as well.

Both assumptions exist because of the psychological phenomena described in this chapter. Therefore, all of us need to assess formal education in light of what we want, and what our core values are. Seeking a "prestigious" or "economically-secure" path, if we don't love and embrace the path itself, will result in disappointment down the road. We might find money, but we won't find fulfillment in our work. Formal education is often a great way to experiment, and find out what we like. What we like will direct our path, and if that path takes us outside of formal education then so be it. We should pursue it with tenacity, and pursue it to mastery. However, formal education is not the only way to experiment, and it is not the only way to find personal fulfillment.

Checkpoint:
The Reasons We Don't Understand Risk

1. Confirmation Bias: we look for evidence of what we believe, and see our world through a subjective lens, discounting evidence that contradicts what we believe.

2. Group Polarization: when people with similar beliefs habituate, the beliefs grow stronger and more extreme.

3. Representativeness and Our Consistent Irrationality: What we think is "typical" of an event impacts our subjective opinion of whether we think that event will occur.

4. The Example Rule: a risk will seem more likely to occur (in our mind) if we can easily recall instances of it occurring under similar settings.

5. The Anchor Rule: any available statistic that we can recall, when considering the probability of risk, will serve as an anchor for us.

6. The Influence Of Our Social Group: we are social animals, we like fitting in. We avoid things that put us at odds with our dominant social group.

Staying Is Way Too Risky
If We Aren't Willing to Commit to Mastery

The risk confusion resulting from these psychological observations is evident when we look at people who remain in careers they aren't passionate about, and they aren't willing to commit to mastery. I come across many people who wish to leave their jobs to pursue entrepreneurial paths; however, they are concerned about the risks. When I inquire as to what keeps them in their current position, as it is clearly not the day-to-day internal satisfaction of what they are doing, nor is it the fact that their position is aligned with their core values. It appears that in most cases their reticence is with respect to the issue of risk and the possibility of failure.

Sometimes we view the current path as secure, and one where a base level of professional competency will allow us to never have to deal with failure, economic setback, or criticism. So even though we have very little day-to-day fulfillment in what we do, we feel that it is the most secure path to retirement. The problem is that this reasoning opens up a dangerous pathway to self-deception, and it is this reasoning that is at the heart of our future discontent when we make this form of rationalization.

We may think that we are secure because we have met the level of entry competency for our profession, and the odds of our making a material, catastrophic, career impacting error is minimal at this point. Basically stay in line, do our time, and we'll be fine. The problem with this belief is that it gives no meaning to the word "work" other than sustenance. There is no greater purpose. There is no intrinsic value. There is no mastery. It is survive, save enough to die, and then die. Pretty depressing to me, and it definitely doesn't trigger a desire for long-term mastery. Most importantly, it doesn't trigger the type of passion that is necessary to do our best and most creative work, and give our most meaningful contribution. It is the nine-to-five punch the clock mentality—uninspiring and devoid of flow.

So why do we often not see the risks in this mindset? From my perspective I find this proposition terribly risky. I am terrified of trading my life for material possessions. I was once terrified that one day I would wake up and be in my fifties, and stuck with the pain of regret that I never had the courage to leave my unfulfilling position, or the logic to at least understand that the "safe" place was actually quite risky. This is why I garnered the courage to leave law. I was also terrified that I was voluntarily foregoing the best, and likely most productive years of my life, in terms of creative energy, drive and the ability to contribute to others, all for a version of economic security. This was a gamble that I was not willing to play. Life was too dear to me. I wasn't avoiding risk by staying at a job that I didn't like. I was actually playing a different risky game. Every option in life involved risk; it was just a matter of which risky path I chose to take—one that led to fulfillment, or one that led to safety.

By staying at the job that I hated I was also betting the house on the gamble that I would actually live past sixty-five, and at that time have the health, desire and ability to actually pursue other things that were meaningful to me. This is a massively risky undertaking. I have no proof that I will actually be content with a typical "retiree's" lifestyle (in fact I am more certain that I won't). Sitting on the beach and playing golf may seem like an ideal prospect for some, but I would argue that it is nothing compared to being in flow. Flow, where one's body, mind, heart, and soul, is voluntarily dedicated to an endeavor, in a way that stretches us and requires all that we have, is far more optimal and fulfilling than any "relaxation" exercise to me. If we had the ability to sit on the beach right now for an extended period of time most of us would find ourselves bored and wanting more after a couple of months maximum.

When we defer passionate engagement now, on a gamble that our engagement in the future will be more worthwhile, we are embarking in very risky behavior. Some of us will defer engagement now because the cost of engagement (perceived risk, fear) is too high, so we will accept our fate, collect our paycheck and repeat the same process over and over each day. Or, in the worst-case scenario, we will defer engagement now because we will allow ourselves to be a product of our socialization. We go to school, so that we can get jobs, so that we can go into debt to buy a house or car, so that we can continue in our unfulfilling jobs, so that we can pay off our house or car, and then save up enough money to comfortably die. Life is survival, ideally accompanied by material comfort, and then death. But it doesn't have to be this way.

When we view life through this lens, it seems amazing the price that we are willing to pay to preserve our economic security. It seems unreal the lengths that we will travel to avoid "perceived" risk. In many cases it means spending our entire working lives in roles that don't bring out our passions, or our unique abilities. It seems that we are willing to give up our entire lives to be safe, but this safety comes at a dear cost. Henry David Thoreau's words, that *the mass of men lead lives of quiet desperation*" has never been more prevalent than today, despite our living in the most technologically advanced society in the history of humankind.

It would be one thing if a job was only a twenty-hour a week engagement, and afforded us the freedom and flexibility to concurrently pursue alternative passions, but most jobs aren't that way. When we combine our normal working week (forty to fifty hours) with our commute time, we find that we have very little time to start a legitimate side venture, other than a casual hobby or entertainment. Casual hobbies and entertainment work well as distractions, but rarely channel flow, and rarely lead to mastery. If we aren't willing to commit to mastery, in what we are currently pursuing, then we need to get out. We need to get out as soon as we possibility can, and as quickly as we can. We need to adjust our habits, and our spending patterns, and our material expectations as soon as we can. Staying is much too risky.

Chapter Four

Embracing Experimentation, Failure, and Leading a Tribe

Redefining the Concept of Failure, Living by "A Thousand Simple Tests"

On July 4, 1845, eight days before his twenty-eighth birthday, Henry David Thoreau embarked on an experiment in simple living using a property owned by his transcendentalist mentor Ralph Waldo Emerson. On the shores of Walden Pond, a thirty-one meter deep lake in Concord, Massachusetts, Thoreau built a modest cabin, where he would spend the next two years of his life, writing, meditating and reflecting on popular society as he saw it. His motivation was not reclusive—he was being intentionally experimental. He had tried his hand at entrepreneurialism, but having discovered that success in commerce required a study of how to make it worth people's while to buy, he at once decided that he would rather study how to avoid the necessity of selling. So he entered the woods in an attempt to be truly self-sufficient—to transact a form of private business. He described his motivations as follows,

> I went to the woods because I wished to live deliberately, to front only the essential facts of life, and see if I could not learn what it had to teach, and not, when I came

to die, discover that I had not lived. I did not wish to live what was not life, living is so dear; nor did I wish to practice resignation, unless it was quite necessary. I wanted to live deep and suck out all the marrow of life, to live so sturdily and Spartan-like as to put to rout all that was not life, to cut a broad swath and shave close, to drive life into a corner, and reduce it to its lowest terms, and, if it proved to be mean, why then to get the whole and genuine meanness of it, and publish its meanness to the world; or if it were sublime, to know it by experience, and be able to give a true account of it in my next excursion[1]

Thoreau saw life as a great experiment that was untried by him, and he admonished his readers to try out their lives by "*a thousand simple tests.*" His account on Walden Pond, first published in 1854 is unique, engaging, inspiring and refreshing. American poet Robert Frost wrote of Thoreau that "*in one book.... he surpasses everything we have had in America.*"[2] After two years in his simple abode, Thoreau left Walden Pond for as good a reason as why he went there, it seemed to him that he "*had several more lives to live, and could not spare any more time for that one.*"[3]

Despite being written over one hundred and fifty years ago, we would think that Thoreau wrote *Walden* as a clarion call for the discontented masses who find themselves in careers and jobs that are unfulfilling. Many of us, because of our fear of risk, cling to the perceived "safe" paths, and never get to experience true flow and optimal experience in a work environment. An interesting observation is that the phenomenon of the "discontented masses" seemed to be just as problematic in the 1850's. Thoreau remarked,

> Most men, even in this comparatively free country, through mere ignorance and mistake, are so occupied with the factitious cares and superfluously coarse labors of life that its finer fruits cannot be plucked by them[4];

He further states,

> It is remarkable how easily and insensibly we fall into a particular route, and make a beaten path for ourselves. I had not lived there a week before my feet wore a path

1   Thoreau, Henry. *Walden, Or, Life In The Woods.* New York: Dower Publications, 1995. Print.

2   Frost, Robert. "Letter to Wade Van Dore." *Twentieth Century Interpretations of Walden,* ed. Richard Ruland. Englewood Cliffs, NJ: Prentice Hall, Inc. (1968), 8. LCCN 68-1448. Print.

3   Thoreau 259

4   Thoreau 7.

from my door to the pondside; and though it is five or six years since I trod it, it is still quite distinct."

We have developed a propensity to establishing well-worn patterns of behavior, and as a result the course labors of life occupy our minds to the point that we often have difficulty experiencing internal satisfaction. It is the same today as it was one hundred and fifty years ago. Although our technology has changed, a similar trap still catches us—the trap of consistency and social conformity. The antidote is embracing a life of risk tolerance, experimentation and passion where our creative drive is so aligned with our core values that our unique voice is heard, and that unique voice provides us with economic security and personal fulfillment, and induces a state of emotional and mental flow.

How to Get Unstuck

So how specifically does one go about getting unstuck? How does one leave their unfulfilling job and start down the internally meaningful path of long-term mastery? It doesn't happen immediately, nor does it happen overnight. Here are some specific action steps to take:

1. What Do You Really Want to Do?

There are annoying and frustrating days associated with any job or business. Don't hypnotize yourself to think that once you make a change that everything will be smooth sailing. Not even close. In fact you may find that what you embark on is actually much harder than you realized, and even harder (in some ways) to your previous job. If you don't plan carefully, you may find yourself in a new job that is only slightly better than the previous one, and looking for a change again.

So where do you start? You start by answering simple questions: What do you value? What is a path worth sacrificing and struggling for? What is something that you are willing, voluntarily, to fight for to get off the ground? What is worthwhile intrinsically, independent of any reward?

In my opinion if you don't nail these questions down, and determine what it is you actually want out of your life, you will just bounce between unfulfilling jobs. Don't for a minute think that you will achieve quick success without some struggle. It is likely to be harder that you think, and you will struggle more, and doubt yourself more, than you even realize. However, when you love the struggle, when you love what you are doing, because it is intrinsically valuable, you aren't looking to bounce the moment things get tough. You stick.

2. Don't Tie Yourself Financially to the Job You Dislike. Build a Couple "Months" Security

I believe that the most common mental barrier to making a change is fear. When it comes to making career changes, fear often manifests itself in the form of financial worry. For example, questions like "what will I do to make money if I quit this job?" and "how will I survive, I don't know what else to do?" ran through my mind when I first got the idea that I wanted to quit being a lawyer. These questions, and variations of them, are very common for anyone who makes a significant career change, especially if the change is from a stable career.

In reality, a change is often the product of several months, even years, of planning and deliberation. At least that was the case for me. I knew I wanted out of law literally several years before I actually stopped practicing. A powerful habit, which I developed during the planning and deliberation stage, was to live frugally. Don't go buy a new car or new house. Don't buy the most expensive clothes. Literally put money away. Put as much away as you can. I used to count the "months" that I could live without a job. The more months I had, the more courage I had to make the change.

3. Even if You Have a Couple "Months" Saved, You Still May Need an Income Before You Launch Your Dream Full Time

Unless you have independent wealth, it is probable that you'll have to continue to work for a while, even if you have a couple months saved, before you can do what you want to do full time. That was exactly the case for our family. After we started our home based business, I still worked in law to pay the bills for another almost two years so that we could save up enough money, and grow our business to the point that I could leave law. We set a very specific income target for our business, and when we hit it, we stuck to our resolve, and I left law. However it took quite a while to hit that income target, and during this time I still had to work in a job I didn't love to pay the bills.

If this is the case for you, then you should also ask yourself whether your current job allows you time to be able to take actionable steps towards what you really want to be doing. Whether it is another business, going back to school, or any creative endeavor, does your current job provide you with flexibility? Are you working 60 hours a week? If so, you may need to take a "transition" job, where your previously developed skills are marketable (even if you don't enjoy using them) but you now have time to pursue a different path. This idea was the primary motivator for me leaving a big law firm to practice law in a small, self directed setting: I would have much more flexibility to build another business.

4. It's a Waste of Time to Feel Sorry for Yourself, but the Temptation Will Be There Anyway. Avoid It.

When I realized that I wanted to leave law I also started, for a time, to feel sorry for myself. I starting being mad at myself for wasting all that time and money going to school for something that I didn't want to use. I really felt like a failure. It hurt my self-confidence big time. Luckily, I snapped out of it. Don't feel sorry for yourself. Get over it. Who cares if you went to school for something that you don't want to do. Who said you had to be perfect when you were 20 and making educational decisions. It is silly. Move on.

5. Put Your Butt Where Your Heart Wants to Be

I would argue that this is the most powerful lesson I've ever encountered in my life. I credit the author Steven Pressfield for teaching it to me. The application of this lesson has done more to eliminate fear, self-doubt, and anxiety than anything else in my life. It also tests whether I really want what I think that I want.

Think about this for a second. If you say your dream is to own a business, why haven't you started a business yet? If you want to be a writer, where is your work? If you want to go back to school, why haven't you enrolled?

Just take one action. One step. Place yourself literally where you think you want to end up. When we decided as a couple we wanted to build a business then we started building. When I decided I wanted to write, I started writing. Results come only after a significant investment of time to develop skill. So no matter where you are, at the present moment, no matter what your current circumstances are, you can start doing what you want to do. If you think that you can't then you don't want it bad enough and you will stay stuck. If you want it bad enough you will start. You will get creative. You will find a way to do what it is that you think you want to do.

6. Embrace Failure. Give Yourself Time.

Ok lets get this one out of the way. You are likely going to fail, at least a couple of times, so get over it. That doesn't mean that you will ultimately fail. You can only ultimately fail if you quit. But you will have setbacks that others around you (particularly those who aren't doing brave things) will look at as failure. They may even tell you such. No matter what you want to do, your exact plan of how it is going to come to fruition isn't going to materialize as you see it. You will end up taking a different route, but that is ok. The most important thing is that you keep your eyes on the destination.

Thicken your skin. Going from where you are to where you want to be will take time. That's ok. Surround yourself with people who believe in you, not people who drag you down, and not people who will criticize, at any chance, what you are trying to do. Odds are they are just insecure because they are living an inauthentic life anyway. It's the tall poppy syndrome. They just want to pull you down. Avoid them.

7. Find a Way to Keep Yourself Inspired Because the Road Is Lonely

This is important. You won't have a coach to cheer you along. You're going to have to self-motivate. I like books and podcasts for this. Here are some of my favorite writers (that keep me motivated and inspired): Steven Pressfield, Emerson, Thoreau, Aristotle, Mihaly Csíkszentmihályi, Og Mandino, Darren Hardy, Tom Peters, Ayn Rand, Seth Godin, Alan Watts, Eugen Herrigel, James Allen, and many more. Find an inspirational reservoir because you will need to tap into it in those many moments where you doubt yourself and your ability to pull it off.

8. When the Appropriate Time Comes, Burn the Ship

At some point you're going to have to go all in. You've got some money saved. You've got your new business flowing a little cash. Whatever is the case, at some point you're going to have to jump. Again (as always) fear will kick in.

I distinctly remember how I felt when I walked away from my office on the last day that I practiced law. It was both incredibly liberating and terrifying all at once. But if you struggle for motivation, burn your own ship. You'll work with more tenacity and drive than you have ever worked in your life. Trust me, and frankly you'll need that type of drive to get what you are trying to launch off the ground. Burn your ship. When the time comes, make the jump.

Checkpoint: How to Get Unstuck

✓ First figure out what you really want to do instead. Don't change jobs for money or status if you don't like what you are doing.

✓ Don't tie yourself financially to the job you dislike, build a couple months security.

✓ Even if you have a couple months saved up, you still may need an income before you launch your dream full time.

✓ It's a waste of time to feel sorry for yourself, but the temptation will be there anyway. Avoid it.

✓ Put your butt where your heart wants to be.

✓ Embrace failure (it doesn't exist anyway). Give yourself time.

✓ Find a way to keep yourself inspired because the road is lonely.

✓ When the appropriate time comes, make the jump, burn the ship.

What Are We Waiting For?
Let's Find, Establish and Lead Our Tribe

The exciting thing is that the Internet, like no other technology in human history, has provided a portal to connect with others, and create value. We are no longer limited to our circle of influence, to where we live, our social or economic background, who we know, or where or what we studied in school. If we have something unique to share with the world, and that unique product, service, or idea can add value to others, then the Internet can not only connect us with others who will benefit from our unique creation, but will also create a portal for us to potentially monetize our passion.

According to well-known marketing expert Seth Godin, the Internet has facilitated a "tribal" revolution, marking a distinct change from the factory model of the past.[5] The Internet has virtually eliminated the previous barriers of geography, cost and time. Therefore, we can connect, establish or link into, a tribe of like minded people who are interested in participating in, and often paying for, our expertise. Before the Internet, it was difficult to get our message or product out to the world unless we were tapped into an established supply chain or power structure. This is what made navigating the traditional educational system so important—it would give us access to the portals that could take our idea or product to the masses. Now the masses are available to all of us within a couple clicks of the mouse. Godin notes,

5   Godin, Seth. *Tribes: We Need You To Lead Us*. New York: Portfolio (Penguin Group), 2008. Print.

Before the Internet, coordinating and leading a tribe was difficult. It was difficult to get the word out, difficult to coordinate action, difficult to grow quickly. Today of course, instant communication makes things taut, not squishy. In today's world, Barack Obama can raise $50 million in twenty-eight days. In the non-squishy tribal world of this decade, Twitter and blogs and online videos and countless other techniques contribute to an entirely new dimension of what it means to be part of a tribe. The new technologies are all designed to connect tribes and to amplify their work. [6]

In addition to the emergence of the Internet, Godin notes three important factors that have contributed to creating an unprecedented period of personal opportunity where we have the leverage to make things happen, independent of our position in society's power structure. First, we have made the realization that a significant portion of our life is spent "working" and that working on stuff that we believe in, and are proud of, is much more personally satisfying than simply *"getting a paycheck and waiting to get fired (or die)."*[7]

Second, there are many organizations that have realized that the factory centric model of producing goods and services isn't as effective and profitable as it used to be. Finally, we no longer automatically direct our hard earned dollars on products and services that were produced in a factory. We now are much more open to unique, innovative and niche products, and products that are influenced by social causes that we can relate to, even if those products have a higher cost. We have used our purchasing power to signal the fact that we will embrace fashion, stories, causes, goods, and services that matter to us, things that we value as individuals.

The former path to growth for a company was to be consistent, trusted, and large. Corporate cultures would resist quick change, because quick change was risky, and risk could lead to failure. This is the factory model that has influenced so much decision-making in our world today. However, as Godin notes, there is a new rule:

If you want to grow, you need to find customers who are willing to join you or believe in you or donate to you or support you. And guess what? The only custom-

---

6   Godin 6.

7   Godin 9.

ers willing to do that, or looking to do that, are looking for something new. The growth comes from change and light and noise.[8]

A Case Study in Tribes: Skype

A perfect example of this principle is the astronomical growth of Skype. Skype is one of the most well-known, and well used, communication methods on the Internet today. Skype is taking a real bite out of some of the leviathans that once held a stranglehold in the telecommunications industry. Our sharing of something we deemed to be of value (a free video telephone service where all we needed was an Internet connection) with our personal network drove Skype's growth.

As a result, a powerful tribe emerged, a movement large enough to make Skype a real player in the communications industry. However this movement would have never happened by corporate maneuvering using the traditional factory mindset. Skype needed the masses to grow. It was the masses that facilitated the growth organically, not the strategies of lawyers and MBAs in corporate boardrooms. To utilize the power of the masses, Skype focused on providing something valuable. Once we recognized this value the growth took care of itself.

Whatever People Are Passionate About: The Makeup of Tribes

A tribe doesn't have to be large to be functional, or profitable. In fact the fundamental notion of a tribe is that it is small. It is the factory model that seeks to provide a low cost (and often low value) good to the maximum number of people. The Internet doesn't care about the notion of maximization in the way that a factory does. Without government censorship or regulation, we control the Internet. The Internet is about us, the consumer. In fact, as the numbers of the tribe are diluted, its appeal to its original members can fade. In order to have a very successful, and profitable, business that uses the Internet as its connector, we are better off to have a smaller group of absolutely loyal followers.

---

8   Godin 18.

Seth Godin illustrates the ability for a tribe to be small, and profitable, through the concept of *"true fans."* A true fan is someone who so deeply cares about us and our work that they will actually invest extra to support us, and most importantly they will share our message, product or service to others in their network. It is true fans that form a tribe. Godin notes,

> A true fan brings three friends with him to a John Mayer concert or to the opening of a Chuck Close exhibit. A true fan pays extra to own the first edition, or buys the hardcover, instead of just browsing around on the website. Most importantly, a true fan connects with other true fans and amplifies the noise the artist makes.... Too many organizations care about numbers, not fans. They care about hits or turnstile clicks or media mentions. What they're missing is the depth of commitment and interconnection that true fans deliver. [9]

To highlight the power of a "true fan" based tribe, Godin cites the example of the now worldwide phenomenon of CrossFit (www.crossfit.com). Greg Glassman, a former gymnast, founded CrossFit in 1995. Using a previously unconventional methodology that promoted broad and general overall fitness, through the use of a variety of weightlifting, sprinting and gymnastics based exercises, CrossFit is now a fully functioning, and economically viable, tribe. It is a movement of individuals, from every walk of life, who are embracing extreme fitness. Through CrossFit, the Average Joes of the world can now feel (and look) like Olympians. There are organized "CrossFit Games" and competitions throughout the world; certification courses, and a growing number of CrossFit certified trainers running newly opened gyms.

One person with an idea, a passion and a vision started all of it. Glassman's idea has since materialized into a significant economic interest and untold personal satisfaction as "The Coach" (as he is referred to by his CrossFit loyalists). However, the way that the phenomenon, and business, grew was not using the "factory system" of distribution. Glassman didn't "push" this idea on us by using mass media advertising to generate brand awareness through "interruption." His tribe grew organically. The tribe facilitated the growth. All Glassman had to do was present a unique value proposition to a small number of people who were connected to others on the Internet, and once those people embraced the value as individuals, they wanted to share it

---

9   Godin 33.

with others. That process repeated itself over and over until we arrived at our current state: a worldwide phenomenon.

We Are Creative, We Have Ideas, We Are Individuals, Let's Embrace It

We may think—all this is fine and good but we aren't unique, and we don't have great ideas to share with the world. If we believe this, I cannot state more strongly that I think we are mistaken. Our current thinking is a product of our behavioral conditioning of the past. This conditioning has taught us not to stick out, not to be unique, and not to be an individual because it is risky. We have been rewarded with carrots for being model and obedient and with sticks for being different. This mindset is the product of the past. Let's become part of the future and break free from this mindset.

Being an individual is only risky in the factory model. We are not living in the factory model anymore. Every single day new ideas are going viral on the Internet. Every single day new businesses and services are being introduced throughout the world. Now is the time that individualism and creativity is rewarded more than any other time in history. Now is the time to embrace the core values that define us as a people. We don't need to penetrate the masses to be successful. We don't need conformity. We only need a tribe, and the more we embrace our unique identity the more loyal our tribe will be.

Now is the time to embrace being an individual. Now is the time to tap into a unique value proposition and create a good, service, message, or idea that relates to a select group of individuals that we can connect to by using the tools on the Internet. We are not limited to the factory model of the past to build a life that is fulfilling and economically sound. We have to be willing to try our idea. We have to be willing to experiment, and share our idea with the world. Our idea or product or service has to be something that others will value. We have to be willing to connect with others, and as others find value in our idea they will share it. A tribe will form around us and we will find ourselves as the leader. At that point we are free from the factory model that has bound us in the past.

What makes us come alive? What is our tribe? What's something unique and valuable that we can create, or tap into, and create momentum using the Internet? We don't need a large advertising budget, we just need to provide value to people and they will spread it themselves. Is it physical fitness like Greg Glassman from Crossfit? Is it bio-hacking and the concept of being a "bulletproof executive" like Dave Asprey and his tribe (www. bulletproofexec.com)? It is the creation of passive income on the Internet using smart, and transparent methods like Pat Flynn from Smart Passive Income (www.smartpassiveincome.com)?

Each of these individuals was able to monetize a passion using the sharing power of tribes. All of these examples highlight the potential of one person with a value proposition. A tribe forms around them, and their value proposition, and the tribe spreads through viral marketing on the Internet. Conventional mass marketing doesn't spread the tribe. Nor is the tribe tactically arranged using high-level corporate decisions making brainpower. There aren't consultants or high-powered attorneys retained to develop brand awareness, and market penetration, strategy. We see value and we spread it ourselves, without needing a reward. This is the time we live in. There has never been a better time to take our idea to the world.

Don't Worry about "Most," Instead Nurture and Gain the Trust of Our Tribe

My wife and I have experienced tremendous growth in our business, and my writing and speaking career has been greatly enhanced by tapping into the concept of tribal power. I use a variety of social media, blogging, and other connectivity methods to attract, retain and nurture a tribe of individuals who are interested in the ideas that I produce. I don't care about what "most" people are interested in. I'm only interested in my tribe. My tribe is the people who are interested in the ideas that I offer. When using the Internet, "most" is not a concept that needs to be focused on. As Godin notes,

> You're not going to be able to grow your career or your business or feed your tribe by going after most people. Most people are really good at ignoring new trends or great employees or great ideas. You can worry about most people all day, but I promise you they're not worried about you. They can't hear you, regardless of how hard you yell.[10]

10 Godin 68.

Godin articulates five actions we need to create and nurture a tribe.[11]
First we need to publish some form of a "manifesto." This is a unifying principle for our tribe. It doesn't have to be long, or even written, it just needs
to articulate to ourselves, and others, what our tribe is about. Next, we need
a way for people to connect with us, a way for the tribe to come together.
This is fantastically simple today through the use of Facebook, LinkedIn or
other social networking groups and pages, blogs, email lists, and many other
methods. The next step is to make sure that followers of our tribe can easily
connect with each other. So whatever connectivity method we use we need
to allow for comments, and group sharing and input. Established tribes take
this action further by organizing group events, conferences or publications.

The fourth step is more of a necessary realization that monetization cannot be the group's primary organizing force. This is counter-intuitive from
the carrot and stick based motivation of the factory model—that all actions
need a specific result. Money will come after, and only after, trust has been
created and the tribe's message has been effectively spread. Value is the currency of trust, and sharing (the dissemination of the tribe's message) will not
take place unless the unique value has been experienced. The last point is
that all of these steps must be done in the public space. There must be ways
for members of the tribe to contribute to its progress and growth.

Author and influential blogger Mitch Joel in his book, *Six Pixels of Separation: Everyone Is Connected. Connect Your Business To Everyone,* describes
the importance of trust in the digital world when bringing people together
to form a tribe (or community in his words):

> Return on investment in the new economy is driven by how loyal and engaged
> your consumers are. Businesses that build trust and engage in their community
> (whether they have created it themselves or take part in an existing one) are seeing
> results and real ROI. Let's assume that you are delivering the ultimate experience.
> Your brand rocks. You offer excellent products and impressive service—you've got
> it all. What's next? You ability to leverage true ROI is going to come from the level
> of trust you have built and the community your serve."[12]

11 Godin 104.

12 Joel 35.

Checkpoint:
5 Actions to Create and Nurture a Tribe

1. Publish a manifesto; outline the unifying principles of the tribe.

2. Make sure that people have a way to connect with us, and a way for the tribe to come together.

3. Make sure that followers of our tribe can easily connect with each other.

4. Monetization cannot be the group's primary organizing force.

5. All these steps must take place in the public space.

Godin also notes six unifying principles when it comes to the creation of a tribe. There must be transparency. Trust is fundamental, therefore we cannot feel deceived, and we are really good at spotting a fraud. The movement must be more than just the person who started it. It must be about something. It must move people and change the way that they think or act. The larger the movement or tribe can grow, the better. In Godin's words "*movements that grow, thrive.*" Another unifying principle is that a movement's manifesto is best understood by how it moves away from the status quo. If a movement is going in the same direction as another movement then that movement won't have the same level of clarity. The last two points are that exclusion is a powerful, and useful, force for unifying members of the tribe and for solidifying loyalty, and finally, a movement is best when it is building its followers up, rather than tearing down those outside of the group.[13]

A tribe isn't formed through coercion, social pressure, or fear. We come together around a shared purpose, or a value proposition that is of interest

13 Godin 105.

to us, or a unique interest that engages us. The exciting thing about this phenomenon is that it doesn't play by the rules of the factory. Obedience, the ability to take orders, memorize and follow, are not rewarded, or held of any great esteem. Social acceptance and consent doesn't matter. Individualism thrives. Exclusion is a unifying principle. We don't need the masses; we only need a few people who value what we are giving enough to share it with others.

When we experience the value associated with a movement, or idea, or product or service that we believe in, we share it with others. Once the sharing takes hold the movement has traction and will continue, provided the rules of tribal retention are maintained. These tribes, connecting and growing, through the medium of the Internet can have powerful economic consequences. Those who are successful in creating, and leading tribes, can be rewarded richly. So not only do they get to engage in a movement that is meaningful to them, they are often rewarded for their courage in starting it.

Re-discovering the Virtue of Failure

I recently visited my seven-year-old son's elementary school and was amazed by the technology in the classroom. It was nothing like my elementary experience—his classroom was filled with laptops, smart boards, interactive computer assisted devices and other gadgets. It was something that I couldn't even imagine when I was seven. I can recall with great curiosity the day I saw my first Atari game console. I used to get so excited to go to my cousin's house because he had a Commodore 64. Things have changed so much since then, but in many ways they are exactly the same.

For the most part, students are taught in a similar fashion. There are memorization heavy tests and report card assessments, teachers often have too many things to juggle and not enough resources to create individualized content where student's unique strengths can be assessed and cultivated. Unfortunately, and the reasons for this are complex and numerous, our schools act as a sorting mechanism. Using its own distinguishing rules, schools sort out the "good" students from the "bad." They sort out the students with a "bright" future from those that are heading for "troublesome" paths. However, their sorting mechanism isn't foolproof. There are many clear examples where they get it wrong.

The schooling system also helps to create, and reinforce, a systemic fear of failure and experimentation. This hasn't changed from the time I was a child. There is the ever-present stick (although these days not as much a literal one), which manifests itself in detentions or punishments for disobedience, poor marks, failing grades for the "wrong answers" and the parent teacher interview to discuss the child's progress relative to her peers. There is also the proverbial carrot—the reward for good behavior, the good marks and positive endorsements for the "right answers." A well behaved child may even be fortunate enough to earn a positive "label," which will follow them throughout their life, such as smart, gifted, talented or advanced. A poorly behaved child, particularly one who is adept at giving wrong answers, stepping out of line, or learning in different ways, may also earn a "label" of a different, and far more troubling kind, given the phenomenon of the Pygmalion Effect.

In the most formative years of their lives, children can become behaviorally conditioned to seek the right answers, get praise from people who are in a position to give it, and avoid inconsistency or disruption at all costs. Failure can be a terrifying prospect for a child. It places children in a position of uncertainty because they are told that their life may be difficult going forward if they don't figure it out. Children with learning difficulties, or a lack of emotional support at home, or in their immediate community, often can't find the resources they need to be "successful" in the conventional school setting. The label that is presented to them, if accepted as the foundation of their self-identity, can have damning consequences that only an empowering contradictory reference can negate.

Also, many students seek career opportunities in post-secondary training that lead to economic security and social acceptance, not individual creativity and personal fulfillment. Getting the carrot, in whatever form it presents itself, feels good, not just to a child but also to an adult. Getting the stick, in whatever form it presents itself, doesn't feel good. The model is effective and efficient. People, like me, who learned how to play the game, come out of the system with sterling credentials, and a "bright future," but (again, like me) find themselves professionally unfulfilled when working in the area they were educated in. This is because we never learned as children to tap into the unique values and abilities that are inside of us. We never learned to experiment with life. We never learned the virtue of failure and risk.

Meanwhile, many people who are rejected by the conventional model, end up innovating, creating, and adding value to the world in a way that changes society for the better. Once they are rejected, or labeled, or "fail" they have nothing to lose. They are freed from the chains of expectation and consistency. No one expects the people who "fail" the school system to amount to anything, so they aren't scared of failure. They aren't afraid to experiment. They aren't afraid to try new things, even if they go wrong. They often experiment until they tap into something unique, and they often change the world.

Learning from the Great "Failures" in Society

Most of us are familiar with the many stories of individuals who failed at first and later went on to great things. Steve Jobs and Richard Branson both found immense personal success and fortune despite "failing" in the traditional educational model. British Prime Minister Winston Churchill was defeated in many elections before ever securing public office. Harland David Sanders (we will likely better remember him by his Kentucky Fried Chicken nickname "The Colonel") had over 1000 restaurants reject his idea to license his chicken recipe. Marilyn Monroe had her contract with Columbia Pictures terminated because she was told that she wasn't pretty or talented enough to be an actress. Jerry Seinfeld's first foray into stand-up comedy led to him being booed off stage. Over twenty-five publishers rejected Dr. Seuss's first children's book. While writing the first Harry Potter novel, J.K. Rowling was unemployed, divorced and raising a daughter on social security. Clearly failure didn't deter these individuals, and there are many, many more examples.

There are many reasons that our current system perpetuates. It is controllable and it is safe. It creates a power structure that is visible and without chaos and uncertainty. It establishes a clear path to who is "supposed" to lead, who is "supposed" to innovate, create or advance society. It is the industrial revolution factory model of education and career advancement. There are plenty of factory vacancies out there in the world that need to be filled. Those who run the factories in our society (the power structures) need model obedient factory workers, and we are conditioned from the time we are children with the carrot and the stick. We are also conditioned to believe that there are certain avenues in life that are relatively risk free—that if we attain a position of status for example, then we won't have to deal with the twins terrors of risk and failure. Our position in the factory system will be secure and we will be able to live out the duration of our lives in peace and pleasure.

It is very natural to have a fear of failure. As humans we don't want to feel less significant than others. We don't want to be separated from our community, even if that separation is in our own minds. It is understandable to intensely fear feeling inadequate because it strikes directly at our feelings of self worth. When we feel inadequate, or less significant, we often feel that "we are not enough." This can be a terribly immobilizing feeling. It can also be very undesirable to feel alone, especially when the isolation isn't self-prescribed as a form of emotional therapy. Failure, when interpreted in a dis-empowering way, can leave us with a feeling of being alone.

Learning to Embrace Failure: The Amateur Scientific Method

All of the negative feelings we associate with failure are made up in our minds. We convince ourselves of the reality of these feelings because of our intense socialization, but we don't need to be terrified of failure. We can condition ourselves to see failure in a different light. We can begin to believe that failure is a process, failure is good, and failure takes us closer and closer to finding our unique voice. Without failure, we may never tap into what makes us unique and great as individuals. If we view life as a series of experiments, all leading to the identification and cultivation of our unique purpose, then failure is not only instructive but also necessary.

If I take a scientific method to my life, failure is not only helpful, it is absolutely necessary. In the scientific method, I start with the premise that I want to accomplish objective X; however, I don't know the exact path to accomplish objective X, especially if objective X is unique and hasn't exactly been duplicated before. Therefore, I will seek input from others who I believe have knowledge of how to obtain objective X. I soon find out though, that despite their input and knowledge, the path is one that ultimately I must discover on my own. In order to discover the path I must gain knowledge and experience, and in many cases I need to try things, not knowing if they will work out. I must fail and learn, fail and grow, learn from my mistakes, gain good judgment from making bad decisions. Under this model there is really no such thing as failure. There are only results. This is a scientific process. If I don't get the result that I want, from an action that I take, then I just change my approach. I continue to change my approach until I get the result that I want.

Why are we so scared of this process? Why do we have no problem applying this model under certain controlled settings (scientific experimentation for one) but resist it in others (like in the planning of our careers and the way that students are taught in schools)? Concerning our societal approach to failure, Kathryn Schulz, author of *Being Wrong: Adventures in the Margin of Error*, notes,

> Of all the things we are wrong about, this idea of error might well top the list. It is our meta-mistake: We are wrong about what it means to be wrong. Far from being a sign of intellectual inferiority, the capacity to err is crucial to human cognition.[14]

"Failure and defeat are life's greatest teachers [but] sadly, most people, and particularly conservative corporate cultures, don't want to go there,"[15] says Ralph Heath, author of *Celebrating Failure: The Power of Taking Risks, Making Mistakes and Thinking Big*. He continues,

> Instead they choose to play it safe, to fly below the radar, repeating the same safe choices over and over again. They operate under the belief that if they make no waves, they attract no attention; no one will yell at them for failing because they generally never attempt anything great at which they could possibly fail (or succeed).[16]

In many cases, the biggest reason that we are terrified of failure is that we haven't engaged the first step in the scientific method—we have no idea what we actually want. We don't even know what we are looking for. We

---

14 Schulz, Katherine. *Being Wrong: Adventures In The Margin Of Error.* New York: Ecco, 2010. Print. 5.

15 Heath, Ralph. *Celebrating Failure: The Power Of Taking Risks, Making Mistakes, And Thinking Big.* Franklin Lakes, NJ: Career Press, 2009. Print.

16 Heath 52.

don't have a clear, concise and compelling objective that we are seeking. We see the objective in general terms and it usually deals with a base level of material comforts, social position, and community significance. So we cling to the institutions that we think will best provide these. The problem is that these institutions rarely provide us with fulfillment. Failure is valuable and necessary when we evoke the scientific method. We determine exactly what we want with clarity and then pursue it using trial and error. Failure is a necessary and valuable part of the process, until our desire is obtained.

Moving Past Fear to Greatness:
Sir Ernest Shackleton and the Endurance Voyage

Twenty seven men had been recruited, many by this simple notice: "Men wanted for hazardous journey. Small wages. Bitter cold. Long months of complete darkness. Constant danger. Safe return doubtful. Honour and recognition in case of success." On December 5, 1914 the crew of the voyage ship *Endurance* left South Georgia headed towards the Weddell Sea. The crew's ultimate destination: Vahsel Bay, where a team of six, to be led by Captain Sir Ernest Shackleton would lead an "Imperial Trans-Antarctic Expedition" across the frozen continent. Shackleton was a seasoned sailor having previously explored Antarctica. When Norwegian explorer Roald Amundsen became the first expedition leader to discover the south pole in December 1911, Shackleton saw one remaining great conquest in Antarctic exploration: crossing the continent from sea to sea, via the pole.[17]

This sense of challenge and adventure spoke to the core of what Sir Shackleton was all about. He was a courageous visionary, and felt compelled to achieve great feats, not just for the pride of his country, but also because of a driving internal need to test the limits of his personal endurance. He once stated "difficulties are just things to overcome, after all." This sentiment would come to define the Trans-Antarctic Expedition as the crew met early ice as they voyaged southward. This early ice slowed the *Endurance's* passage, eventually causing the great sea vessel to become frozen fast in an ice floe.

Realizing the severity of the situation, Shackleton ordered the crew abandon the ship in February 1915. A temporary camp was established on the ice

17   Worsley, Frank. *Endurance: An Epic Of Polar Adventure.* New York: W.W. Norton, 1999. Print.

and the crew waited, breaking the monotony by hunting seals and penguins. The crew's rations were stable as they were able to get much of their supplies from the ship. Shackleton had hoped that the ship would eventually be released from the ice and they could work their way back towards Vahsel Bay. However, in October 1915 icy water began flowing in, and shortly thereafter the once sturdy ship submerged into the sea's black depths.

The crew was now in a very precarious position, and as an astute leader Shackleton knew that, in this frozen prison, human despair was just as dangerous as the moving ice below their feet. They established a temporary camp on a large flat ice floe, hoping that the floe would drift towards nearby Paulet Island, where additional rations were located in whaling camps. After multiple attempts to march across the ice failed, the crew was running short of rations and hope. There was a steady supply of seals and penguins for meat and fuel, but they needed to come up with an escape plan soon or else their brave intentions would be in vain and the entire crew would perish.

On April 9, 1915 the ice floe they had been camping on broke into two. Shackleton ordered the crew onto three lifeboats they had salvaged from the *Endurance* and they headed toward the nearest island. After five nightmarish and exhausting days at sea the men landed on Elephant Island, nearly three hundred and fifty miles from the shipwreck. Elephant Island could only be a temporary stay or the crew would perish, as it was far from shipping routes and it was nothing more than an inhospitable mass of ice and rock. In an act of courageous desperation Shackleton decided to risk his life in an open boat journey 800 nautical miles to the South Georgia whaling stations. A tiny, 20 foot lifeboat, which they christened the *James Caird,* was reinforced with additional improvements to make the daunting journey and together with six of the bravest and most able sailors, Shackleton launched off Elephant Island April 24, 1916.

For more than two weeks this frail vessel tossed against the strong winds, vicious waves and icy chill of the sea, constantly in danger of capsizing, but the crew persisted, undeterred, and eventually landed on the unoccupied southern shore of South Georgia. Rather than risking another dangerous sea voyage Shackleton decided that a land crossing of the island, where they could meet up with Norweigan whalers on the other side, was the most prudent course for the crew's rescue. Leaving three to camp behind, Shackleton and his two most trusted companions, conquered mountainous terrain for 32 miles and 36 hours until they finally reached the whaling station at Stromness on May 20, 1916.

All of Shackleton's men were eventually rescued, with Shackleton himself returning to Elephant Island for the last survivors. Although the land passage of Antarctica was never completed, Shackleton, and his crew's bravery, leadership, and heroics have been continuously celebrated as one of the twentieth century's greatest feats of endurance, persistence, resilience and determination. His leadership tactics and abilities have been studied in business school and written about in many books. His commitment to attempting a great challenge, and the way that he responded to difficulties, brought out his inner greatness.

Each of us has inner greatness, but for many of us this greatness will stay dormant. It will never be unleashed. It will never even be tested. Very few of us will attempt a literal voyage of Shackleton's magnitude, nor will we have to deal with the types of physical and mental hardship that the crew of the *Endurance* experienced. If we want to find out what is inside of us, if we want to channel whatever greatness we possess, we must first decide to attempt something difficult and challenging. We must place ourselves, consciously, into a difficult endeavor. Our inner greatness is not unleashed in a comfortable routine. We need a challenge to bring out the greatness that is inside of us. If we have ever wondered what we can endure, what we can accomplish, what greatness is inside of us, we will never know unless we embark on a great challenge, and commit to that challenge with as much fortitude and determination as Shackleton and his men.

There are opportunities for challenge all around us. We can take a risk and build the business we have always dreamed about. We can learn that new skill that will change our prospects. We can heal that relationship. We can overcome that difficulty. We can conquer that fear. Let's take the challenge head on, channel our inner greatness. A great challenge may bring with it pain, and it most certainly will bring fear. But if we never try, we will never know the greatness that is inside of us, and we can never truly become empowered.

Chapter Five

Reinvention: Our Digital Self

The Internet Has Created a World of Possibilities for Us

The Internet, and its unprecedented ability to connect and create relationships, share meaningful ideas, products and services, and form tribes of like-minded, value-driven, individuals, has opened up a world of possibilities for us outside of the conventional factory schooling system. When we take the time to determine what we uniquely value, make decisions and set goals based on these values, and channel flow and mastery in our activities, we have the ability to create unique value for others and thereby direct our own life in a meaningful way. This is an exciting prospect.

This message, as a whole, is very different from the message indirectly portrayed by the factory schooling system. In the factory system failure is to be avoided, and career experimentation is much too costly to attempt. In the factory system the future is bright for a few people. A few people are the innovators. A few people hold the power. It is reserved for those who successfully navigate the system. The Internet however, is giving power, and a bright future, to the people who are able to create value for others and form a tribe. The power of a tribe is that it spreads a message, and it spreads it virally.

The Internet has completely changed the way that we connect with each other, the way that business is transacted, and the way that we exercise our purchasing power, create and endorse fashions and trends, and share information. The reality of the Internet however is that it can also facilitate a number of unique challenges and obstacles when seeking empowerment and reinvention in our careers. The most prevalent is the nature of the digital fingerprint that we both intentionally and inadvertently create for ourselves.

Our Society of Trackers and the Creation of Our Digital Doppelganger

We have become a worldwide, interconnected, society of trackers. Many companies are widely known to track our purchasing history, and use sophisticated algorithms to predict our future buying preferences. Other companies will sell user data and information to marketers who are looking for niche groups to introduce their products. Facebook and other social media websites will track, archive and interpret our user data to make intelligent judgments on the type of products or services that should be advertised to us. Corporate tracking habits on the Internet are facilitating an important public conversation on the nature of privacy, and the question of what we actually own as individuals (such as the rights to our images, or the rights to the ideas we create or produce on the Internet).

We have developed a bit of a self-tracking obsession. Nora Young, author of *The Virtual Self: How Our Digital Lives Are Altering The World Around Us,* notes:

> What are people tracking? Everything, basically. If you can think of a behavior to track, you can probably find people who are tracking it, and a website that facilitates it...There are websites to track your fluctuating mood, your sleep habits, your exercise patterns, and even the people you have had sex with (including how long it lasted, and how it was for you—rated with a star system).[1]

We can now easily track our exercise routines and running patterns. There are websites that allow us to track our dietary habits, along with our progress towards personal pursuits and individual goals. Pinterest (www.pinterest.com) allows us to build virtual pin boards where we can "pin" things that are interesting to us. It also allows us to "project" interests, and

---

1   Young, Nora. *The Virtual Self: How Our Digital Lives Are Altering The World Around Us.* Toronto: McClelland & Stewart Ltd., 2012. Print. 12.

track the things that we would like to have, do or experience in our life—a form of digital "self-visualization" or "dream board" tool.

Personal blogging has become commonplace, and on blogs, along with our personal and professional networking profiles, we can track the books we are reading, the videos we are watching, the images we are viewing, the concepts, links, articles, or ideas we are "liking" or "sharing." We share the videos and songs that we appreciate, as well as the links of articles we are reading, or podcasts we are listening to. There is a trend that everything in our life can be tracked, and also readily visible to others, including those outside of our immediate network through social media websites.

Twitter, and other real time "status update" websites even allow us to track our thoughts. These may be random, poignant, irrelevant or irreverent. It doesn't matter; all that matters is the fact that we can now share. We "follow" others whose thoughts we think are follow-worthy. We are "followed" by people who consider our thoughts to be follow-worthy. Not only this, but our thoughts, in the form of updates, are now tracked as to "where" those thoughts took place. Facebook, Twitter and other social media sites allow for applications that track, and publically post, where we are at the exact time that we have a particular thought, or decide to share a link, idea, video, or picture with others.

This tracking phenomenon—something that was completely impossible only ten years ago—serves to create a self-directed "digital fingerprint." This digital fingerprint creates a picture of who we are—and it is broadcast to the world and to ourselves. Nora Young continues:

> The pattern I see emerging is one where everyday information about where we are going, what we are doing, how we are moving, and how we feel is brought together in the creation of a digital picture of ourselves. It's a picture that combines the intentional and the unintentional. Compiled into a Data Map, it gives us one (though not the only) strong depiction of who we are. The representation of who a person is becomes the vast amount of data the person generates. [2]

All of this serves to create a form of "digital doppelganger," a narrative, created by our online tracking that forms an image of who we are, where our interests lie, and what we are about as individuals. It serves as a signal to

---

2   Young 27.

the world, offering up our "story," a picture of our "actual" behavior, documented in a complex, way. It becomes our digital fingerprint, and it impacts not only how others view us, but also how we view ourselves in the world. As author and blogger Mitch Joel notes,

> Now, more than ever, people's first interaction with a brand is happening at the search box. That first page of search results defines you. It defines your brand and either taints you or teases the consumer to push on and read more, comment, or get others' perspectives.[3]

How We Are Defined on the Internet: The Power of Self Perception

The influence of self-image on our actions and psychology is well researched and well documented in academic, self-help and human performance literature. It is also widely known that many life and sports performance coaches, as well as personal counselors and therapists, will use self-image re-creation and visualization conditioning with their clients to help them make significant changes in their life.

In self-help literature millions of books have been sold which focus on this subject, including the widely popular *Psycho-Cybernetics* by Dr. Maxwell Maltz.[4] Dr. Norman Cousins is famous for lecturing and writing on the effect that belief can have on our ability to fight illness; while performance guru Anthony Robbins, through his books *Unlimited Power*[5], *Awaken The Giant Within*[6], and his widely popular fire-walking seminar "*Unleash The Power Within*," uses self-image visualization techniques, based in Neuro-Linguistic Programming (NLP), to help us change the "story" that exists in our head.

The general premise in self-image therapy is that our self image, or mental picture that we have about who we are, and how we should act, forms

---

3   Joel 6.

4   Maltz, Maxwell. *Psycho-Cybernetics: A New Way To Get More Living Out Of Life.* Englewood Cliffs, N.J.: Prentice Hall, 1960. Print.

5   Robbins, Anthony. *Unlimited Power: The New Science of Personal Achievement.* New York: Simon & Schuster, 1986. Print.

6   Robbins, Anthony. *Awaken The Giant Within. How To Take Immediate Control Of Your Mental, Emotional, Physical & Financial Destiny.* New York: Summit Books, 1991. Print.

the foundation upon which our entire personality and behavior is built. This self-image is based on our beliefs that we have about ourselves, based on our socialization, our mental references created by past experiences, interpretations, successes and failures, and the intentional affirmations and directions that we use on our own accord. The general foundation being that our actions will not deviate from the self-image that we hold. This self-image has tremendous pull. It is mental super-glue that keeps our actions consistent with the mental picture of how we think we should act.

We may talk about wanting to be an entrepreneur for example, or daydream about owning our own business, or embracing a different career, but if we have some sort of block in our self-image (such as severe risk aversion) then we won't take action. If we think that we are risk adverse, or unable to really build a business, or survive outside of the "comfortable" job that we have obtained in the factory system, we will not take action, no matter what our desire, or the discomfort of our current situation. It is like revving the engine with the parking brake on. No movement will take place.

As a result, our digital fingerprint, or "data story," that we have created on the Internet, when embraced as our self-image, can act as a hypnotic trap about who we are, and how we are supposed to act. Our mental "story" is a summation of social conditioning, beliefs, as well as the results and consequences of prior actions and decisions. This "story" serves as an impediment to embracing experimentation and risk and reframing our understanding of failure. The digital fingerprint that we leave behind through our social media profiles can reinforce this story and keep us psychologically trapped in a disempowering setting because we begin to believe we are incapable of wholesale reinvention.

I have seen this play out in the lives of people who feel "trapped" in an unfulfilling career. Over the years they have created a self-identity largely based on a digital fingerprint that is objectively constructed to manage risk. If we look at their profile on professional networking sites it tells the story of a successful professional or executive. Their "networks" are largely based on associations that they have made in a professional setting.

Even though they may want to change their career, and reinvent themselves in a new, more empowering, frame of reference, to do so would involve a wholesale re-creation of their digital personality. This re-creation would be visible to others, who may contact them and wonder what is going on. This is inevitable for the people who take the courageous step and seek reinvention. Many others will simply rationalize. They will tell themselves, "this is who I am," "this is what I went to school for," even though they find no fulfillment in their career, and there is very little potential for fulfillment in the future because what they do is antithetical to their unique core values.

Our Digital Self Image:
Are We Open to Experimentation or Are We Mitigating Risk?

Another danger in this self-generated digital fingerprint, is that we can create a digital self-image that is a functional tool, a machine, an object designed to constantly mitigate risk, rather than a unique self-image, open to experimentation, and embracing failure as a learning instrument. An example of this is evident in an interview conducted by author Nora Young, with Paula Gardner, associate professor in liberal studies at OCAD University in Toronto and the co-director of the mobile experience lab.[7]

Professor Gardner researches bio-mapping, the process of creating two and three-dimensional objectified maps based on our biometrics. Her focus is on critiquing the way that we think about all the personal data that we are producing (a large part of which is produced through self-tracking), and why we will often unquestionably accept the self-image that our data presents. Concerning Gardner's observations Young notes,

> Her take is that a particular sort of "biomedical discourse" has been taken up in the culture, coming to us from the psychiatric science in particular. In its popularized form, that discourse equates the self with the brain, and reduces the brain to what is computable. As she put it to me, the way this medicalized view of the self is simplified in popular culture suggests that 'if you know [the individual] through biomedical science or psychiatric science then your mood is computable; your personality is computable.' The full richness of human personality is flattened, by reducing it to that which can be subjected to computation. [8]

If the self has been objectified, or flattened, then it can be adapted, and refined, and continually perfected as a tool against any danger that may

7   Young 188.

8   Young 190.

be exist. This "perfectible self" is similar to the "disengaged subject" that philosopher Charles Taylor wrote of in *Sources of the Self: The Making of the Modern Identity,*

> The growing ideal of the human agent who is able to remake himself by methodical and disciplined actions…what this calls for is the ability to take an instrumental stance to one's given properties, desires, inclinations, tendencies, habits of thought and feeling, so that they can be worked on, doing away with some and strengthening others, until one meets the desired specifications.[9]

What are the primary areas where we want to "adapt" and "perfect" our digital self? It is in areas relating to what has constantly been on our minds since we were children—economic security and social acceptance. We are encouraged by our parents to stay in school and obtain degrees so that we can be employable. Our teachers encouraged us to get the best grades because our grades would translate in the future into the safest, most secure and highest paying jobs. The media constantly reminds us of how difficult the economy is, and our employers help to remind us of how grateful we should be just to have a job, no matter how unfulfilling it is. As a result, it is common to see us shape our professional networking profiles to be as objectively impressive as possible, which serves to mitigate against any risk of economic uncertainty.

Defensively Shaping Our Digital Footprints: How My LinkedIn Profile Hurt Me

The need to shape our image in the most socially and economically impressive fashion possible is readily identifiable by how we sometimes use professional and business-networking sites like LinkedIn (www.linkedin.com). Reid Hoffman and a group of Silicon Valley entrepreneurs, including some of the key players responsible for the successful establishment of Paypal, first launched LinkedIn in 2003. The founding group's vision was to create a social network portal that would cater to the professional world.

---

9 Taylor, Charles. *Sources of the Self: The Making of the Modern Identity.* Cambridge, MA: Harvard University Press, 1992. Print. 159.

Although its power as a business-facilitating engine is evidently clear, Facebook, by many users, was initially viewed as a personal social network, not one that a serious businessperson or professional could reasonably establish mutually beneficial relationships or transact business. Facebook, and prior to that MySpace, also didn't provide a clearly organized database for job searchers, or a means for employers seeking qualified workers to search out candidates in an effective fashion. LinkedIn, among other things, is an attempt to solve these deficiencies.

At the time of writing, LinkedIn has over 175 million users in more than 200 countries, offices in most major commercial centers in the world, and according to the press page on its website, new professionals are signing up to join LinkedIn at the rate of two new individuals per second. This makes LinkedIn the largest professional network on the Internet. The company is a publically traded entity and sources its revenue from providing hiring, marketing and consulting solutions to companies and individuals, as well as the securing of premium paid memberships from its users. LinkedIn has also grown through acquisition. It acquired Rapportive: a browser plugin that takes contact information from other social networks like Facebook and Twitter and places them into Google's Gmail. In addition it recently acquired Slideshare, the "YouTube of slide shows," an innovative social sharing portal for PowerPoint and other presentations.

LinkedIn is a tremendously valuable resource for us to network, build relationships, make connections, do business, and seek out opportunities. It allows us to "connect" with other people and form associations based on similarities such as having previously worked together, currently working together, having transacted business together, or just simply friends. The site uses a "gained-access" approach, where any new connection must involve a real relationship (for example having worked together, gone to school together or identifiable as a friend), or the intervention of a mutual contact (an "introduction"). Also, the invitee of a connection request must accept each connection, and the invitee may report a new connection request as "spam" or "I don't know." Too many spam or unknown reports can result in account restrictions or closure. As a result, an environment of trust is facilitated on the site.

LinkedIn also allows us to join and form groups that may be of interest to us, relating to particular industries, specializations, interests, or ideas. Therefore it perfectly facilitates the creation and maintenance of the "tribal" movement as previously discussed. Groups are collaborative in nature, where information, articles, conversations, blog posts, and networking and professional events, are listed and shared. This allows us to not only expand our personal connections but also learn new skills and information at the same time.

LinkedIn's most noticeable feature is that we can build, and publish, a digital resume. This resume is viewable by our connections as well as the general public (according to the our privacy settings). We can showcase particular work or community experience, skills, education or knowledge. Our connections can endorse us for our abilities and provide written recommendations. Our profile serves as a real time lens into our professional capabilities and accomplishments, including our reputation amongst our peers and others that are familiar with our work or business. LinkedIn profiles also take on an "aspirational" tone as we can specifically list what we are interested in, or the skills or positions that we are looking for. Profile building can be a wonderful way to maintain a professional edge and since profiles are part of LinkedIn's searchable database they can also lead to many new job and partnership opportunities for us when headhunters come calling.

The innovation associated with providing this form of connectivity on a professional level has created a massive value proposition, richly rewarding the founders of the company and those who had the foresight to invest early. However, something that is rarely discussed is the tremendous pressure that these user generated, peer enhanced, digital profiles create to keep an individual from embracing career and life experimentation. I saw this both with my own profile that I created prior to my decision that I needed to leave law in order to find fulfillment. I also see it in the current profiles of many people who I know are not fulfilled in their career.

While I was practicing law, I had taken up the cause of maintaining my user profile with meticulous detail, highlighting all of my law related skills and accomplishments. The marketing directors and partners at the firms that I worked at encouraged this habit. It would have been hard to tell how discontented I was in my legal career by viewing my LinkedIn profile. The need for job and economic security can motivate us to project an image that will maintain safety. In the case of my profile, I had highlighted all of the many accomplishments, commendations and skills associated with my training and practice as a lawyer. The need for economic security, and social acceptance, motivated me to create and project a digital self-image that was a form of user-generated fiction, at least from an emotional perspective.

This user generated fiction, this distorted digital fingerprint, had very reinforcing consequences on my emotions and psyche, it also had real consequences on the way that I was perceived. I was a "lawyer," I was not a writer, and I was not a businessman or entrepreneur. My friends and family knew me as a lawyer. This was also the very real digital projection that was evident if someone searched for me on the Internet. Sometimes, when I had a particularly bad day in law, I would look at my profile on the firm website, or on LinkedIn, and I would say to myself, "no, this is what I do, this is what I am, even if I'm not happy."

But it wasn't who I was. It wasn't what I did. It was a user-generated fiction that I had created to preserve my economic security. I wanted to make myself look as employable and desirable as possible. It was a life that had been born from my factory education and then reinforced by my user generated digital profile. The image had been influenced by what others at the firm did. I used their model as a model of job security, and therefore I modeled my user-generated profile after theirs.

I struggled in this battle for too long before I realized that the digital self-image that I was projecting to preserve my job security was actually a major contributor to my discontent. I was trying to fit my actual feelings with the feelings that should be associated with the image that I created. My digital self-image however was not a function of reality; it was based on what I thought I should project in order to preserve my security. It was based on the influences, perceived and real, of the people who I believed held the fate of my job security in their hands.

Our Digital Self Image Projects a Story to the World: Let's Ve Who We Really Are

The digital fingerprint that we create projects an image of who we are, and what we are capable of, in the minds of other people who have access to us (if we allow for a public profile then this includes the entire online world). This definition follows us wherever we go. It serves as a publically accessible live journal. Once a digital fingerprint is left behind in the "public forum" it is essentially impossible to remove. Those who are closed and guarded, and venture only into the shallow waters of social media exposure, are protected against this type of privacy invasion. However, they miss out on the potential for tribal growth that the Internet presents to spread products, ideas and services in viral capacity.

I know many small business owners who resist a Facebook page, who think Twitter is silly and useless, and who never engage in any form of consistent blogging or social media exposure. As a result, these businesses miss out on huge marketing opportunities. They miss out on the chance to establish a tribe, and have the tribe spread their message for them. Conventional "push" or "interruption" marketing tactics bind them. They have to buy space to interrupt people. Their only hope in growing a business organically is through non-web based, word of mouth. This was a very impactful form of marketing before the Internet, and it still serves as an effective means on a micro level, but it doesn't facilitate rapid and viral growth the way the Internet does.

The challenge for many small business owners and people wanting exposure for their product, service, idea or movement is that the more "real" that a person can be, the more effective their message will be to a potential tribe. Exclusion is a fundamental organizing principle of a tribe. By definition, an exclusive group isn't for everyone. The exclusion that takes place in Internet based tribes isn't the form of external exclusion we are used to seeing, such as the inability to attend a private school or a country club.

Individuals, their choices, and their preferences control the Internet. Institutions and organizations do not control it. We can choose to join whatever tribe we wish. We cannot be institutionally excluded because of a certain characteristic or lack thereof. People from every background rally around a cause, product or service to form a tribe. Therefore, the exclusion takes place in that we also choose not to be engaged in the tribe. The essence and power of the tribe is that it is polarizing. We don't need, or want, everyone to join our movement. We don't need, or want, everyone to purchase our product, service or idea. What we have isn't for everyone.

Therefore, in order to highlight our individuality, in order to create our unique value proposition so that we can influence tribal movement, we must be willing to allow exposure into what we are about, whether that be a brand, business, idea, movement or individual. Trust is the currency of choice. Our tribe has to trust us and our brand or product, and we will have a more difficult time establishing trust if we are unwilling to open ourselves up, if we are unwilling to create a digital fingerprint. However, the moment we start to create this fingerprint, our life becomes traceable. Potential investors, partners, and employers, can "Google" us and find out what we are about (or at least what the Internet says we are about).

Being Real Has Consequences: But Be Brave, It Is Worth It

Everyone is aware of the dangers of inadvertently posting evidence of an indiscretion, a sketchy photo or video, or an inflammatory or controversial tweet or blog post, if the posting results in sharing, which takes the indiscretion forever out of our control and places it in the public domain. There are also subtle dangers that can impact us socially. When I left law I was very active in the blogging community. I publically stated what I thought about the conventional billing model that lawyers cling to, about what I believe is a lack of leadership and innovation in large firms, and about the many young lawyers that I was aware of who desperately disliked their profession but who felt trapped, and didn't know what to do to create a new empowering future. My blog posts were not inflammatory, they were not defamatory; however, they were brutally honest (in my opinion), and because they were brutally honest, they connected in a real way with some people. My most honest blog posts were the ones that were most frequently shared, re-tweeted, or commented on the various social networks that I use.

My honesty had consequences. On a positive note, it helped me to establish a tribe. I was contacted in private by people who expressed appreciation for my honesty, and they felt like I was telling their story, and they continue to follow my writing. They told me that I inspired them. They thanked me for my example and for the hope that I gave them that they didn't need to just accept, as a given, the life that was in front of them. Just because they had made it through the factory system and arrived at the point where they found themselves didn't mean that they were stuck there. They still possessed the power to re-create their own identity. They told me that my example, and courage, and the public nature of my confessions were inspiring and liberating for them.

However, there were other consequences of which I am very aware. I was not fired from my job because of ineptitude or laid off because of a weak market. I left on my own volition because I came to the empowering realization that I was chasing someone else's dream. I realized that my career was not aligned with my core values. I realized that I had arrived at my destination not because I wanted to go there but because I had given the most decision-making weight to the values of security and social acceptance. As a result, I had allowed myself to get swept with the tide. I realized that I had not determined exactly what I wanted out of my life at an early age, and I had not pursued it. I had sought the path that would bring the most economic security and social acceptance (in my perspective).

By going public with my true feelings about what I was doing, I drew a line in the sand and intentionally stepped over it. I publically stated that I didn't want the life that I had worked so hard to obtain, and I let people know, including my former employers (who were connected with me through my LinkedIn and Facebook profiles, who could freely read my blog, and who could receive my tweets) that I believed that there were many others like me who felt the same way.

As a result, I was no longer part of the "group" that I had worked to penetrate. I was now an outsider, albeit intentionally. I could no longer rely on the security and comforts that the group could offer. I could no longer lean on the crutch of security to avoid having to make hard decisions. The reality was that if I failed in my new ventures, I would be a public failure, and I would also be on my own. I would have to chart my own path from here on out. It would be very difficult for me to ever return to the big firms, even if I wanted to, despite having a sterling record during my tenure. By leaving the group, and announcing my displeasure in a public forum, I intentionally alienated myself.

This is both the opportunity and the difficulty of the world that we live in. We can build trust, grow businesses and establish a brand or message that is engaging, influential, and eventually profitable by using social media and connectivity tools, but in order to do this we have to be willing to go public with our individuality. We have to be willing to be exclusive. We have to be willing to be criticized. We have to embrace exclusivity in order to tap into the power of a dedicated tribe. When we do this we are bound to be controversial. We are bound to offend certain people. So if our primary consideration is security, and we are concerned that any public displeasure derived from a posting that we did will impact our ability to make a living, we will keep quiet. As a result, we will miss out on the power of a tribe.

Powerfully Honest (Even if It Offends Some): The Joe Rogan Experience

A perfect example of the power of exclusivity on the Internet to attract and retain a tribe is the *"Joe Rogan Experience"* a very popular podcast by former *Fear Factor* host, current stand-up comedian, and Ultimate Fighting Championship color commentator Joe Rogan. Since December 2009, Rogan has hosted a consistent, engaging podcast, broadcasted live and archived on his website at www.joerogan.net.

Rogan has produced over 400 episodes. The format of his podcast is very unique. It is a conversational format, with no predetermined show topic or time restraint. His shows will generally last between two and three hours, although he has many shows that are shorter than this. However, on the average, his shows are very long in comparison to other popular podcasts. Because it is conversational, with no specific time limit, he is able to delve deep into the beliefs of his guests on a wide array of topics. It's like taking a three-hour bus ride with interesting people, and engaging at times in random, humorous, and deeply intelligent conversation.

He consistently produces interesting shows, collaborating with a wide variety of compelling guests, covering an incredibly diverse array of topics. There isn't a pre-set format for the show. There is no time limit. He doesn't use a script, or a pre-rehearsed set of questions. The essence of the podcast is that it is a conversation, unscripted and unrehearsed. No fancy studios, no fake hosts. The interview is broadcast live, and a video archive is available on Rogan's website as well as a download on iTunes. It is real, at times hilariously real, at other times poignantly real, and potentially offensively real. It is how real people talk to each other in their living room, away from cameras. However, it is taped, and available for free to the entire world, and hosted by a well-known television personality.

Rogan's format is clearly unique, but what is even more interesting is that Rogan embraces controversial issues and methods. He will use incredibly colorful and explicit language, which will automatically turn off a large number of people. He makes his personal positions very clear, including his strong opposition to draconian government measures and corporate corruption. He will not shy away from openly endorsing controversial, even illegal products, or issues that he supports. For example he frequently endorses the use of marijuana, mushrooms and other psychedelic drugs and makes reference to his usage habits. In fact, he will often acknowledge being under the influence of marijuana during his show. He will openly endorse controversial products such as nootropics, memory enhancers, and intelligence and cognitive enhancement supplements.

Like Rogan, his guests are individualistic, compelling, at times inspiring, always real, sometimes quite humorous, and at other times very controversial. He has hosted an incredibly diverse range of personalities such as BALCO founder, and former convict, Victor Conte who was the focus of the U.S. Federal Government professional baseball steroid witch hunts in the early 2000s; "Freeway" Rick Ross (Ricky Donnell Ross), a convicted American drug trafficker who presided over the largest cocaine empire in Los Angeles in the early 1980s; Rock singer, and wine producer Maynard J Keenan; Egyptologist, lecturer and natural science expert John Anthony West; accomplished ultra-distance marathoner and raw food advocate Rich Roll; reporter and media whistleblower Amber Lyon; UFC Champion Georges St. Pierre; controversial comedian Andrew Dice Clay; American anti-war activist and former Marine Adam Kokesh; and television personality and self-appointed "Sasquatch Expert" James "Bobo" Fay.

Rogan is in the public eye. He is a television personality, yet to a casual listener, he has complete disregard to the potential ramifications of his positions to his public persona. Many people would think that taking such an endorsing position of controversial, even illegal, products would hurt his career prospects. Quite the contrary—his unapologetic individualism, yet very empathetic nature, has made him a more compelling figure. It has attracted a very loyal tribe. His podcast is one of the top podcasts on iTunes and outperforms (in terms of the total number of viewers) many cable television programs.

His podcast is not just an episode in controversy, a segment of rude and off-colored humor, for the sake of being controversial. His podcast has many moments of genuine and real human caring, where Rogan and his guests embrace topics like "happiness bombs" (anonymous charitable giving), human fulfillment, flow psychology and optimal experience, educational reforms focusing on empowering youth, and the power of positive belief systems.

People who question the nature of his methods have missed the point completely—a point that Rogan obviously understands, and masterfully embraces. The Internet is the ultimate forum for exclusivity and individuality. The more that we can become exclusive and embrace our unique individuality, the more we are able to connect with others in a real way, the more we are able to establish a loyal following, and the stronger our following, the greater our influence. He is a public persona, because he has embraced his individuality. People can relate to him. People trust him. He is real. People feel his sincerity, and as a result they tune in and share it with their friends.

Are We Attracting Our Tribe? If Not, Why Not?

By writing my real feelings, in spite of the potentially negative professional ramifications, I was attracting followers and building trust. I would write boldly and bluntly that I felt people who stayed at unfulfilling jobs were making a mistake, and that the real issue was the absence of self-honestly and courage, not the existence of prudence and rational decision-making given the uncertainties that exist in the job market. But by being honest I was being polarizing, and I was attracting attention. I was pushing away those people who remained discontented in their careers.

I am only interested in connecting with the few, and I know unequivocally that the few exist. I know it. Many of them have contacted me. There are a number of people, the "few," who weren't served well by the factory schooling system. They are the "few" that did all the right things, got the right degrees, got the right jobs and still find themselves disengaged and confused about the continuation of their professional life. They may hypnotize themselves with short term comforts through material pleasure but they miss out on long term engagement because their core values are not aligned with what they spend the majority of their time doing.

These "few" may read a book by Seth Godin, or may have one of my blog posts shared with them, and may even fantasize about a reinvention. They may think about the power of the Internet to launch a new business venture and engage a passion, but because they have to be "real" and an "individual," and because this has to be done in the public forum, where the wrong people (for example their current employers) can potentially view it, they are often immobilized in implementing their idea.

I have talked with many people who dream of setting up a side business, or even a blog, to engage a passion and hopefully, over time, pave the way to an engaging career. When I ask them simple questions like, "Well, have you set up a blog yet? Are you writing? Are you making videos? How are you connecting with people? How are you spreading your message?" How are you creating your tribe? The answer is usually that they have done nothing, other than to think about it, and watch others who are actually taking action. Also, in many cases they don't want their "hobby" to be overly visible because their employer may not approve of it.

The reason that they feel paralyzed is because of fear. In some cases, particularly the lawyers or those in the corporate world, they have signed some form of contract where they covenant to spend all of their material time in the service of the company or law firm. What is crazy is how this non-compete is interpreted. I know many lawyers and corporate professionals who are spending consistently fifty plus hours a week in the "service" of their employer. Even with this significant contribution they feel that if their "side-engagement" is subjectively interpreted by the powers that be in the organization (those individuals who usually hold power are the ones who have shown the greatest proficiency in alienating their entire life to the consecration of the organization) as too much, then they jeopardize their own job security.

As a result, the portal for engagement, and potential liberation, the Internet, is right in front of people, but sometimes they fail to effectively use it because it could potentially signal "disloyalty" to the institutions that are controlling them if they are too visible in their efforts. The factory system will not become the path to liberation in their life. The factory system becomes their forever controller and they are never free.

They had to comply in elementary and high school to "get in" to college and university. Then they had to comply in college and university to secure a job. Now they have to hold their job to maintain their security, to keep their house and to survive. For many people this process is never fully engaging. They never get to feel what it feels like to stay up late at night because they want to, not because they have to. They never get to feel the excitement of a unique challenge. They never wake up in the morning excited for what they are about to create. They never embrace the positive side of experimentation and failure. They are the "few" but they are real. They are the ones that I want to help. They are the ones that this book is written for.

A New Form of Currency: Reputation Capital

The Internet has created a new form of currency—a digital commodity referred to as "reputation capital." What reputation capital attempts to quantify is the value of the reputation of an organization, entity, or individual within a particular context, community or setting. Perhaps one of the best examples, and arguably the first form of reputation capital on the Internet, is the seller rating system that is used on the world's largest online auction site, www.ebay.com. Selling on Ebay is very easy—we open an account, create an ad, and start an auction. There are no barriers to entry with respect to utilizing this platform to sell our goods. For a lot of potential customers this could present a risky proposition.

The existence of online financial clearing services such as www.paypal.com decreases the risk of credit card fraud; however, for the novice user there is still an initial sense of trepidation when buying something over the internet, from a complete stranger who may live on the other side of the world, without first having the opportunity to see or test out the goods. What Ebay fully understood is that the user community would work to create a risk mitigating system on its own.

We like giving our feedback. We like our voice to be heard. So on Ebay we can rate our purchasing experience based on our perception of the seller's accuracy in the item description, communication methods and effectiveness, speed of shipping and reasonableness of processing fees. Therefore, when Ebay endowed us with the ability to rate sellers on a one to five star basis, they knew that we would utilize the principle of reputation capital to sanction (in the form of negative ratings) poor quality sellers and reward (with positive endorsements) good ones. These ratings would serve as a risk-mitigating signal to future customers to avoid the bad sellers (in turn causing these sellers to leave the platform all together).

Reputation capital is a tremendously valuable tool in the world of online commerce. One of the challenges that producers and retailers face when selling products and services online is establishing trust with customers. A company, organization or individual with a high degree of reputation capital will generally have a high degree of online trust. This online trust can be communicated to potential customers through publicly listed, group indicated, rating systems. So when a potential customer is looking at purchasing a product or service from a new retailer they can look at the previous reviews, ratings and comments that other people have provided, with respect to the retailer, and determine whether they want to enter into a transaction. This is critical on the Internet, which is full of scam artists, and fly by night marketers looking to make a quick buck on a cheap product or an unsuspecting dupe.

Reputation capital is a two edged sword. On the one hand, a company or individual who works hard to provide a value added product or service, who is sensitive to customer needs, and who generally works to build a "quality" business will (conventionally) receive positive feedback, testimonials, rating and reviews. These reviews will be publicly accessible to potential customers and will likely influence these buyers to purchase the company's products or use the individual's services. However, a company or individual who provides a poor quality product or service, a negative customer experience, slow shipping times, or in the worse case scenario actually defrauds customers, will receive very negative reviews, ratings and feedback. These reviews will also be publically available to potential customers, and will likely influence them not to use the services or purchase the products.

Therefore the moment we choose to do business online we are subjecting ourselves to the force of reputation capital. As a result, retailers and producers have to continually focus on adding value and enriching the customer experience because a negative review online, particularly one that is outside of our control, and is repeatedly being picked up by the search engines, can have a lasting damaging effect on our business prospects. A negative opinion on the Internet, with respect to our product or service, also has the ability to reach far more people because of social media. Having a disgruntled customer is far more dangerous now than it was thirty years ago to a business because that customer can project his voice to thousands using online forums, groups and social networks.

The Internet provides a built in safety net for companies or individuals who try to manipulate their ratings. External online forums, relating to just about every sub-niche we can imagine, exists on the Internet. Here people share opinions and reviews based on their experience. The algorithms of the popular search engines pick up these forums and the various terms and keywords that are used on them. There are also many specific sites that have been created and designed to produce user generated reputation capital. For example, at the time of writing by typing the search string "rate my" into Google, I can quickly find page specific rating sites relating to employers, doctors, lawyers, teachers, landlords, and IT service providers. It is clear that we like to use our "voice" on the Internet and one of the most powerful ways to exercise our voice is to rate the services, products and experiences that we have and share our ratings with others.

When a potential customer is researching a product or service, one of the first things they will do is "Google it," or go to their favorite search engine and research what people are saying about the product. The search engine generates links and hits that include the forums, not just the actual company website. Therefore, a retailer of goods, or a producer of services cannot manipulate their reputation by generating false positive reviews. The comments on the public forums will show up in search engine results and will be visible to potential customers. Further, search engines are becoming increasingly sensitive to user-generated content, social media influence, and are becoming almost foolproof in determining what is a real review.

This user generated reputation capital is not merely words on a paper of some obscure ranking website. Arguably the second largest search engine in the world is YouTube. People en mass are taking to YouTube to voice their opinion on absolutely everything. Videos can put a face, and emotion, to a product or service (both negatively and positively). Next time we are on YouTube type in the words of a product that we know and see how many reviews we will find online. It is amazing—like an unpaid army of product reviewers and testers. All of which goes to form the reputation capital of a product.

Clearly, the idea of reputation capital is a valuable addition to the world of online commerce. It mitigates risk by creating user-generated rewards and stigmas, thus sorting good and trustworthy sellers from lower quality, and even devious, retailers. This concept is permeating online marketing and making its way into the careers of professionals as well. The idea that "our reputation precedes us" has much greater ramifications online than it does in the real world. In fact, these days, it is hard to separate the real world from the Internet, if such a separation is even possible.

Our Digital Brand Is What Google Says It Is

An individual's reputation is a function of perception as much as it is of reality, and as Chris Anderson famously noted, *"your brand is not what you say it is…it's what Google says it is."*[10] This concept goes far beyond the notion of a product based "brand," or a service based "brand," or a corporate based "brand." It applies just as readily to an individual "brand," or the way that potential employers, investors, and partners perceive us with respect to our career. Our personal reputation capital will form the basis for many career and business opportunities that will come into our life.

Rapper Jay-Z once famously stated, *"I'm not a businessman, I'm a business, man."* This concept doesn't apply to celebrities, athletes and musicians anymore. Every single one of us has a reputation that will precede us online, and that will form the basis for how we are perceived by others. Therefore all of us are "businesses" in a general sense, just like Jay-Z. The value of our personal "business" is really the value of our reputation capital. Personal reputation capital is creating an economy of trust online, not just in commerce but also in relationships as well, particularly relationships as they apply to career opportunities.

10 Joel 6.

Writer and consultant Rachel Botsman is the co-author of the book *What's Mine is Yours: The Rise of Collaborative Consumption*[11], and is a founder of the *Collaborative Lab*, a innovation based organization focused on helping start-ups, established businesses, and local governments use collaborative consumption to deliver innovative solutions. Botsman's research delves into the concepts of online trust, reputation capital and the power of collaboration and sharing through social networks, and how these concepts will transform business, consumer decisions and generally how people live and associate with each other. In a speech at a TED conference in 2012 Botsman discussed in detail the concept of reputation capital and its implications for the future.[12]

In her talk Botsman made a very convincing case that our online reputation will be our most important asset going forward. She uses innovations such as www.airbnb.com (a website that allows us to rent out our houses, apartments and other spaces to strangers from all over the world), www.doliquid.com (a website that allows us to rent out our bicycles), www.taskrabbit.com (a form of Ebay for errand running where we hire strangers to run errands for us), and www.lendingclub.com (a peer to peer financial lending site where we can enter into private loans with each other), to make the case that reputation capital is creating a marketplace for goods where no marketplace once existed.

Were it not for the trust that is created through online reviews, and reputation capital, we would not be willing to engage in these types of transactions; however, with the Internet not only are these transactions taking place, they are thriving and adding massive value. As she aptly notes *"virtual trust will change the way we trust each other face to face."* Virtual trust, through reputation capital, allows complete strangers to engage in transactions.

Botsman goes on to further describe the implications of reputation capital on individuals and their careers. She notes *"reputation is the measurement of how much a community trusts you."* She also identifies, as I have previously

---

11 Botsman, Rachel and Roo Rogers. *What's Mine Is Yours: The Rise Of Collaborative Consumption*. New York: Harper Business, 2010. Print.

12 Botsman, Rachel. "The Currency Of The New Economy Is Trust" *TED*.
<http://www.ted.com/talks/rachel_botsman_the_currency_of_the_new_economy_is_trust.html.> Web. 12 June 2013.

noted, that each social network posting, forum comment, transaction record that we make online goes to form the basis of our digital image (what
she calls a *"reputation trail"*) that impacts our personal reputation capital,
thereby projecting to a particular community whether, and in what form,
we should be trusted. Although context clearly matters when establishing
reputation, Botsman suggests that perhaps in the future our reputation from
one community could be transferrable, or at least influential, to another. She
suggests that the future could make way for a *"Facebook or Google like search
and see a complete picture of someone's behaviors in different contexts over time."*
This would enable complete strangers to easily see who has trusted us over
time, and why.

Botsman believes that reputation data has the potential to, if not completely replace the traditional resume, then at a minimum serve as a highly
influential indicator of trustworthiness to potential employers. In support
of her position she points to www.stackoverflow.com, an online community for computer programmers where technical questions are asked and
answered by fellow programmers. As questions are correctly answered users
obtain points, or ratings from other users on the site, and are even listed in
the user section based on their rankings, with the top ranked users showing
up first in the profile. Botsman notes that computer programmers are starting to list their stackoverflow rating on job applications, and that employers
are recognizing this as a form of trustworthiness and credibility as to their
skills as a programmer.

Reputation Capital Leading to Risk Paralysis: Increasing the Cost of Failure

Botsman's points are all valid. She makes a very strong case for the power of
reputation capital to act as a credible barometer of trust, and even bridge the
gap between our digital and non-digital lives. Reputation capital is a valid
and useful concept, as it applies to building customer trust in an online
purchasing experience, creating and cultivating markets that were previously
non-existent, and creating quantifiable signals for determining a person's
reputation and reliability within a particular community. The only danger
of reputation capital is the way that an individual interprets their resultant

reputation scorecard, and whether it's existence serves as a deterrent to experimentation and taking risks.

Reputation capital is a phenomenon tied to another trend—everything is documented, and can be recalled at a later time. As a result, some people are "digital ghosts" refusing to join social networks and participate in online communities because they value their privacy, and they don't want to leave a digital fingerprint. This stance is very hard to maintain as the world moves towards the integration of the Internet into our everyday life. Today it is very rare for someone not to have some form of an Internet profile. So for those of us who do participate online, the fact that everything is documented, can be a deterrent for "putting ourselves out there," experimenting with a blog or YouTube video series, or answering questions online, like in a stackoverflow forum. This is because we may not want to generate a "negative" reputation in these contexts that may follow us and potentially damage us down the road.

By tracking everything we are doing, and allowing for publicly archived negative feedback (in the form of ratings, or other peer created data) we are increasing the cost of failure. When the cost of failure increases, we become less inclined to risk, and we stick to the safe paths. For many this means staying in careers that are unfulfilling, rather than risking a negative reputation that may follow us in the future and impact our economic security. The reality is that we often need to fail in order to find out what we really want, and what we are uniquely good at, and what brings us individual fulfillment. But if we are never willing to risk failure, for whatever reason, we won't tap flow, fulfillment and mastery. There is a direct relationship between our willingness to fail and our ability to achieve mastery over time.

There is nothing that one can do (short of boycotting the Internet) to reverse the trend of reputation capital. It is what it is. It is important however that we don't become so fixated on avoiding criticism online that we are never willing to experiment with life. It is important, to our long-term fulfillment that we are willing to try new things, even if by so doing we receive a negative review. It is through trial and error that we learn. It is by receiving negative reviews that we are able to correct our mistakes and obtain positive reviews. It is by getting outside of our comfort zone that we find what we truly value and want to master. If we are terrified of a string of failures following us forever on the Internet it is likely that we will stick to what we know, regardless of whether it is fulfilling or not.

Checkpoint:
How to Create a Powerful Digital Presence

✓ Our personal brand on the Internet isn't what we say it is, it's what Google says it is.

✓ The essence of an Internet tribe is exclusivity. Don't be afraid to be "powerfully honest."

✓ We have to become unique creators of value added information.

✓ Being real has consequences, but it is the only way to build trust and draw people to us.

✓ Are we attracting and nurturing our tribe? If not, why not?

✓ Reputation capital is a powerful tool on the Internet, and acts as a trust regulator, but we can't let it prevent us from taking risks and reinventing ourself.

Chapter Six

Thrive:
Channeling Our Inner Creative Genius

We Cannot Force Our Product or Message on Anyone, We Must Create Value

The Internet is full of scammers—marketers, who attempt to use antiquated methods to interrupt, manipulate and in some cases even deceive us into purchasing their product or service. Online marketers often make claims that are not only audacious, they're harmful, because of the message they are portraying. For example, I recently saw a Facebook advertisement directed at small business owners that offered the prospect of using social media to *"double the size of our business without ever having to talk to a customer."* Imagine that! Using a forum that is designed to create connections to double the size of our business and never have to deal with the "burdens" associated with making a real connection and providing good customer service.

Popular social media websites can be an effective portal for deceptive marketing practices like false and misleading claims in an attempt to "trick" us into visiting a website. The enforceability and traceability of lawsuits relating to Internet based deception has not kept pace with the speed that the deception has proliferated. However, the Internet has a built-in safety mechanism. It is called trust and the power of individual choice. The wonderful thing about the Internet is that deception doesn't work over the long run. Someone may be able to dupe us in the short term (which is often all these marketers are after), but the practice is ultimately ineffective.

No matter how large a company's marketing budget is, and no matter how intelligent their executives and attorneys are, they cannot force, or trick, us to pay attention to them on the Internet. We always have the power. There are no exceptions. We can simply choose not to click on a web page. We can exit out of a site without any consequences, and we never have to come back. Even if a marketer engages in a deceptive practice like using images unassociated with their product to tacitly endorse a product, once we figure out what is going on, we will exit the page. That is the best-case scenario for the deceptive marketer. In the worst case, we lose trust, tell our friends, and use the same social media engine to drive negative sentiment towards the deceptive marketer.

This is very different from life before the Internet, where push marketing tactics allowed a marketer to hold captive an audience (if we could afford the airtime), and information was in short supply. So if someone on TV or the radio told us it was true, we rarely doubted it. If we were watching our favorite sporting event, listening to a Presidential debate, or enjoying our favorite sitcom, unless we planned on literally leaving the room or turning off our TV, at each commercial break we were held captive to whatever product or service purchased our attention. The jingle line for the product conditioned us to think about it whether we wanted to or not.

A captive audience hearing a repeated message doesn't realize that there might be other alternatives and choices available in the marketplace. Also, with limited access to information we can't refute the claims that the marketers make regarding their products. Our frame of reference for a particular product was what we had heard on the radio, or television, read about in a limited supply of magazines or newspapers, or heard from a work or business associate, trusted friend, or family member—who were all gaining their information from the same isolated reference sources. In many cases choice wasn't even a real option. The supplier may have had a near monopoly on the product, given the costs and time associated with shipping.

Today is a radically different consumer environment. Conventional network television has been replaced by on demand digital cable where we determine exactly what we want to see, when we want to see it. Technology allows us to skip every commercial and never be held captive. Traditional radio is being countered by commercial free programming options where for a set fee we can take the power back. And above all else, the Internet dominates as the pre-eminent source of choice, information and the engine that powers trends. Today, choice is the norm. Information is everywhere and generally that information is available for free. With a simple combination of search engine queries we can find the good, the bad and the ugly about whatever we are looking for. Then, with the click of a mouse we can securely purchase our product, and have it shipped to our doorstep at a very low cost.

We cannot succeed in today's Internet-based marketplace by forcing our self and our size on others. The conventional notion of power doesn't work the way it used to. To succeed on the Internet we have to be able to provide value to others. It's not nearly as important "who we know," because even large power players cannot force a viral trend on the Internet. Viral trends are independent of power structures. Viral trends are created when a niche market, or as Seth Godin labels it a "*tribe*," believes that something is valuable enough to share with other people that they know. It can be the endorsement of a product, service, or even something funny or random like a meme or a video. We deem something to be of value when it connects with us in a unique way. Once this connection is made we want to share it with those in our network.

Now Is the Time to Create Value and Share Our Unique Voice

In order to create an economically viable business in today's marketplace we don't need to have a large marketing budget to interrupt people and hold them hostage with our product. We have to have an idea, product, service or message that adds value to a group of like-minded individuals who then share our message with other like-minded individuals in their networks. The most exciting reality is that we don't even need to get our message or service or product out to the entire world. We just need to find a tribe. We just need to get it to a group of people who are valued by it. The value that we give them will trigger the sharing process.

Now is the time for us to start creating unique value. This process is at the heart of the personal empowerment themes throughout this book. Once we discover what we intrinsically value, and once we commit to mastering it, then we are on the path of creation. As soon as we start the creative process, our unique contribution will be noticed and over time, shared. To help us understand the process I will share three case studies of individuals who, through the discovery of their unique values and passions were able to create massive value for others.

Value Creation Case Study #1: Changing the Way We Learn

Salman Khan had a secure and prestigious job as a hedge fund analyst at Connective Capital Management when he took up the task of tutoring his cousin Nadia in mathematics. Khan had great proficiency in math having completed several graduate degrees in electrical engineering, computer science and business at The Massachusetts Institute of Technology (MIT) and Harvard respectively. Using a simple medium, Yahoo's Doodle Notepad, Khan created a series of easy to understand and follow, instructive videos on the concepts that Nadia needed to learn.

The videos were unique. They were on a black background and used white or neon colored "doodles" or diagrams that explained the concepts. Khan wanted to de-emphasize the importance of the classroom in regards to learning. He thought it would be most effective to duplicate a person walking through a problem using a simple piece of paper. He also wanted to create tutorials that could be paused, since a classroom lecture could not be. In an interview with USA Today in 2008 he noted, *"If you're watching a guy do a problem (while) thinking out loud, I think people find that more valuable and not as daunting."*[1]

Clearly of unique value to Nadia, the videos weren't originally created for mass distribution; however, they were incredibly effective. Many people considered them much more effective than the traditional classroom mode of delivery. So when other friends and family members came to Khan, asking for similar assistance, he decided that he would upload his videos to

---

1   Associated Press. *USA Today*. "Need A Tutor? YouTube Videos Await." <http://usatoday30.usatoday.com/ news/education/2008-12-11-youtube-tutoring_N.htm> Web. 20 June 2013.

YouTube, and make them publically available, so that they could be easily shared with others.

What has transpired since 2004, when Khan first started his videos, can only be described as remarkable. Salman Khan's simple, instructive videos have generated more than 300 million hits on YouTube, and have attracted well over a million subscribers—making his channel one of the most powerful and influential sources of educational content in the world. All of his videos remain free and available in real time. His videos have generated more hits than the open content of many of the top American Universities combined, including many prestigious Ivy League Universities, where it would costs many thousands of dollars to learn the same lessons.

Salmon Khan quit his hedge fund job in 2009 to focus on creating tutorials full time. Khan Academy (www.khanacademy.org), the name of the non-profit website that Khan launched to house his tutorial videos has a stated mission of *"changing education for the better by providing a free world-class education for anyone anywhere."* Also available on his website are practice modules and exercises where problems are generated for students to solve based on certain skill levels and performance. The website also has the ability for tutors to coach students and track their work. It also includes many volunteer opportunities for people wanting to assist in the translation of the lessons or spread the academy's message throughout the world.

The tutorials have expanded beyond mathematics to include lessons in history, healthcare, finance, physics, chemistry, biology, astronomy, economics, cosmology, organic chemistry, American civics, art history, macroeconomics, microeconomics, and computer science. The lessons are also being made available in 21 different languages. Multiple educators, engineers, advisors, professionals and instructors have joined the Khan Academy non-profit team to change the face of modern day education and as they state on their home page *"learn almost anything for free."*

His passion has attracted the attention, and funding, of some of the most powerful technology companies and minds in the world. Khan Academy has the financial support of the Bill & Melinda Gates Foundation. On September 24, 2010, Google announced on their official blog that they would donate $2,000,000, as part of their Project 10^100 program, to the Khan Academy to *"support the creation of more courses and to enable the*

Khan Academy to translate their core library into the world's most widely spoken languages."[2] In 2011 it received a $5 million grant from The O'Sullivan Foundation, founded by cloud computing innovator Sean O'Sullivan, directed at expanding the teaching faculty; extending content through crowd sourced contributions (a la Wikipedia); and developing course content to help users blend virtual and physical learning.[3]

One individual, who was able to tap into his core values (love of learning, desire to teach, ability to create innovative learning methods), to create a unique value proposition (simple instructive videos), started all of this. His unique value proposition went viral. When people experienced value in the tutorials, they shared it with the people they cared about. People started to talk, and with the power of connectivity of social networks, combined with the ease of use of YouTube, there was tremendous leverage to spread his videos.

Now Salman Khan is seen as a visionary, an innovator, and an educational guru and celebrity. He has been featured on CBS's 60 Minutes, PBS, National Public Radio, CNN, the BBC, Wired Magazine, in multiple newspapers and in numerous national and international publications. He has appeared on Charlie Rose, The Colbert Report, and in 2011 presented a highly influential TED talk. In April 2012 he was listed among Time Magazine's 100 Most Influential People for 2012. There is no question that Khan is a brilliant innovator, but we also have to recognize the power that is unleashed when a unique value proposition is embraced and shared using social media. That is the true story behind Khan Academy.

Value Creation Case Study #2: A Regular Guy Talks Wine

Gary Vaynerchuk understands the viral power of the Internet to build personal and consumer brands as well as anyone. At only 37 years of age, Vaynerchuk is a *New York Times, Associated Press* and *Wall Street Journal* Best-Selling Author, with his books *Crush It! Why Now Is The Time To Cash In on*

---

2   Google Blog News, <http://googleblog.blogspot.ca/2010/09/10-million-for-project-10100-winners.html> Web 24 August 2013

3   Tech Crunch <http://techcrunch.com/2011/11/04/the-osullivan-foundation-grants-5m-to-online-learning-platform-khan-academy/> Web 24 August 2013

Your Passion[4] and *The Thank You Economy*[5]. He has close to a million followers on Twitter. He is a regular keynote speaker at entrepreneurial, online media, and business marketing conferences. He has delivered a TED talk. He is a regular on media outlets having been featured on everything from Late Night with Conan O'Brien and The Ellen DeGeneres Show to CNN, CNBC, NPR and MSNBC. He was listed in Decanter Magazine's 2009 Power List, which profiles the most influential people in the wine industry, and he was also one of www.askmen.com's "Most Influential Men of 2009." As Co-Founder and CEO of VaynerMedia, Vaynerchuk helps Fortune 500 companies like The Campbell Soup Company, PepsiCo, and Green Mountain Coffee, and professional sports franchises like the New York Jets, and the Brooklyn Nets, create digital brand presence using social media.

Vaynerchuk wasn't always this influential. His story is a perfect case study for this book. Vaynerchuk's education and social background didn't give him any advantages in the online world (or non-online world for that matter). Originally from Belarus, his family immigrated to the United States in 1978. As a young man times were tough and money was tight. When his family first arrived in Queens, New York their first home was a studio apartment that housed his family and also his grandmother and great-grandparents. Within a few months of their arrival, Gary's father's (Sasha) construction job, which he had arranged before the move, disappeared. But his parents were driven, hungry, entrepreneurially minded, and willing to do whatever it took to build the life for their family in America that they had dreamed of in Belarus.

Sasha Vaynerchuk found a job as a stock boy in a liquor store in Clark, New Jersey and it didn't take him long to work his way up and become a manager, eventually saving enough money to purchase his own store. He was able to later purchase another store, "Shopper's Discount Liquors." Vaynerchuk jokingly suggests in his first book, *Crush It: Why Now Is The Time To Cash In On Your Passion,* that the store *"looked exactly what you think a Shopper's Discount Liquors should look like."*[6]

---

4   Vaynerchuk, Gary. *Crush It: Why Now Is The Time To Cash In On Your Passion.* New York: Harper Collins, 2009. Print.

5   Vaynerchuk, Gary. *The Thank You Economy.* New York: Harper Business, 2011. Print.

6   Vaynerchuk, *Crush It*, 19.

As is the case with most family businesses, Gary learned the ropes (perhaps against his will at times) bagging ice, dusting shelves and manning the cash register. When the store was slow, he would flip through the pages of *Wine Spectator* magazine. Although the store was not known for its fine wines, and the bulk of their sales were from hard liquor or beer, Gary, at a young age, started to realize the "cultural cachet" of wine. Also, unlike the hard liquor buyer, a wine consumer was usually open to influence in terms of the brands that they would purchase. He notes,

> I started to notice a pattern: people would come in to buy their Absolut or their Johnnie Walker and I knew that I or any staff could talk until we were blue in the face about the other brands, they were still walking out with their Absolut or their Jonnie Walker…The wine buyer, though, would often walk in looking a little lost and spend ten minutes tentatively peering at labels as though hoping a bottle would jump out and spare them from making a decision.[7]

Since the wine customers were open to suggestions, Vaynerchuk knew there was an opportunity, and on November 14, 2005, his thirtieth birthday, while driving on the New Jersey Turnpike, he had his ultimate "aha" moment. He had noticed that sites like MySpace and Flickr and YouTube were becoming popular. These sites had nothing to do with business, but were about people sharing things they found interesting with other people. There it was for him. He would launch a video blog to build an online wine community. In February 2006 www.winelibrary.tv was born.

Vaynerchuk understood the power of the Internet to develop brands and create communities. Intentionally, winelibrary.tv was not created to sell wine. This is something that traditional entrepreneurs sometimes struggle with when using the Internet to promote their brand or product. They feel that time spent on an indirect marketing endeavor, one that may not result in direct sales, or even worse, giving away something for free, is a waste of time and money. As a result, they default back to the "push" marketing concepts that they are familiar with, such as buying ad space to directly promote a product or trying to convince someone why they should buy them and not the competitor.

---

7   Vaynerchuk, Crush It, 24.

However, Vaynerchuk knew that push marketing didn't have viral power. People would share what they valued. So he decided that he would be the "*wine guy*" and he would "*tell it as it is,*" instead of "*spouting the same classic terminology every time, how the bouquet was rose petals or the finish was silk.*" He states, "*I would stick my nose in my glass, suck in a mouthful of air and wine, and the only thing running through my head would be, 'Man, this really tastes like Big League Chew' or 'if this isn't a Whatchamacallit bar, I don't know what is'.*" He was trying to take an experience that many people found frustrating or unfamiliar, and make it familiar and fun. It worked.

His unique and individualized approach, really just a matter of cutting through pretention, telling it as he saw it, and being real, created a viral trend. His video logs, describing wine in "common language" became very popular with a tribe of consumers that could relate to the confusing wine buying process. He connected with a community. The community found value in his message and they shared his videos. Not only did his family business thrive (and significantly reduce their advertising budget in the process) but Vaynerchuk became a bit of an Internet celebrity, with media, book writing, speaking and consulting engagements just around the corner.

He never went to school to become a "marketing expert." He does not have a fancy MBA from a prestigious school. He simply followed the model as described in this book. He was authentic. He created a unique value proposition that was embraced by others. His value proposition was shared using social media channels, thereby creating a community of loyalists. This is the power of the Internet to create new careers.

Value Creation Case Study#3:
Turning a Layoff into a Value Driven Purpose

The beginning of Pat Flynn's story is exactly the same as many others. Armed with a newly minted B.A. in Architecture from the University of California, Berkley, Flynn took a job at a local Southern California architectural firm. The reality of being a nine to five worker sunk in really quickly as he realized that his ability to create wealth, in his career, would be limited by the amount of time that he would be willing to give. Time is finite, and also zero-sum. Therefore, time spent working would mean time away from the other things in his life that he found meaningful. This is a predicament that many workers face. Many of us accept this reality so we embrace the vacation and short-term respite we are given from our employers and try to make the best that we can with our lot in life. Like myself, Flynn had a hard time just accepting this premise as his default reality.

He had read books, like Tim Ferriss's popular *The Four Hour Workweek*[8] and started to dream what life would be like if he could duplicate his "active" employment income, with passive, automatically generated income through the Internet. It was not that he disliked his job, he just knew that the "factory model" of getting an education, getting a job, working the job, and saving the best he could, would likely never allow him the freedom to live a life that he considered truly fulfilling.

On October 17, 2008 Pat started a blog, www.smartpassiveincome.com, and penned his first post, a short, empowering piece entitled, "Why I Will Quit My Job For Passive Income." In the post he discussed the power of the Internet to create passive income streams, and how a passive income stream was the best method of liberating him from the chains of employment, thereby allowing him to embrace a life of freedom and engagement. He started writing blog posts describing how people could make passive-income on the Internet, while they were at work, detailing the steps that he was specifically taking to slowly create freedom from his nine-to-five. The blog was not designed with the end result of "making money," but rather it would serve as a journal where he could track his passive income progress, and create a community of followers.

At the time the blog was launched Flynn had experienced modest success in creating automatized income streams on the Internet. To advance his architectural career Flynn had resolved to take the LEED (Leadership in Energy and Environmental Design) Exam. To help him study for, and pass the exam, Flynn had created a simple blog where he could organize his notes. That way he could study from any computer or mobile device (like on his lunch break at work), without having to haul around his books. All he needed was an Internet connection and he could access his exam prep notes.

8   Ferriss, Timothy, *The 4-Hour Workweek: Escape 9-5, Live Anywhere, And Join The New Rich.* New York: Crown Publishers, 2007. Print.

He was surprised one day when he received a message from a stranger who had been following his blog. This individual thanked him for the wonderful notes he had provided because they had helped him to prepare for his own exam. Intrigued at the thought that others were following him he decided he would do a little investigation into who else was monitoring his blog. He downloaded some tracking applications and found out that there were over 300 unique visitors a day to his site, most of which were being referred by search engines like Google. He also saw that the visitors spanned 14 different countries and 23 states. Then the entrepreneurial bug bit him.

He thought that since his website was being trafficked, perhaps he would monetize it. He had heard about programs such as Google Adsense and other affiliate marketing programs where he'd receive a commission if someone bought a product by clicking on a link sourced from his website. He started to implement a few strategies and soon started making modest, but real passive income. He then set his sites on a specific goal. He would continue, in his spare time, to implement Internet based passive income strategies until he was making enough money to leave his nine-to-five and really "live" his life the way that he wanted.

It was then that reality kicked in, and not in a way that he was expecting. Despite his Ivy League education, and having passed the LEED Exam, he was unexpectedly laid off from his job. The "traditional" model hadn't provided him any long-term security. So instead of dusting off the old CV and trying to find another "job," he decided that there was no better time than the present to go after what he really wanted—absolute freedom through passive income.

He made the bold decision to pour his entire self into creating passive income on the Internet. His LEED Exam site had now spun off additional money-making products (such as a study guide in the form of an eBook) and he had a modest income flow to at least pay the bills. Despite this, he was still on a risky path, and there was no certainty that he would be able to pull it off. For many people the fear and uncertainty would have been too much, they would have just struggled to find another nine-to-five, even if their heart yearned for something else.

Flynn was different; he dove into this new life adventure with zeal. Perhaps as an act of positive self-analysis, or the desire to create a community for support, he also made a commitment to his smart passive income blog readers that he would share his progress in how he was doing making money online, and he would also give away, for free, all of his money making tips and strategies. To create further trust and transparency he also decided that he would create "Monthly Income Reports" where people could see exactly how, and where, he was making his money online.

His policy of transparency was brilliant. With the implementation of a few search engine optimization steps, Flynn's smart passive income blog found it's way towards the top of the many search engine inquiries of people, like Flynn, who were working their unfulfilling nine-to-fives and trying to create a path to freedom for themselves through passive income. When visitors came to his site, and saw not only his transparency, but also his candidness, and when they recognized the value of his strategies, they came back.

They also began to share his site with their friends. With respect to this tendency, I can speak from personal experience, having used Flynn's free Internet marketing strategies many times to significantly increase the revenue in my own business, I have subsequently referred many people to his website. I frequently refer people to his website because he has created a unique value proposition (the specific steps on how to market a business online, for free). The content that he gives away for free is the exact content that search engine and Internet marketing consultants often charge hundreds of dollars an hour for.

Flynn is now widely considered an "Internet marketing guru." His smart passive income blog is one of the most visited blogs on the subject. His smart passive income podcast has had more than 2,000,000 downloads, and is profiled as one of the top five financial podcasts on iTunes. He has been featured on Fox News and led a panel at the Blog World Expo in New York City in 2012. Recently he was profiled in *Forbes* magazine as one of ten "Leaders Who Aren't Afraid To Be Transparent."[9] All of this by using the pattern that has been shown repeatedly in this book—one person creates a unique value proposition, based on something that interests them, and it is

9   Forbes. <http://www.forbes.com/sites/johnhall/2012/08/27/10-leaders-who-arent-afraid-to-be-transparent/>
    Web. 24 August 2013.

embraced and shared online by a community organized around a common interest.

There Is Creativity Inside of Us: Here Is Why It May be Dormant Right Now

Some of us, having read the stories of Salman Khan, Gary Vaynerchuk, and Pat Flynn might be thinking, "sure, it's easy to read about exceptional people who do exceptional things, but I'm just an ordinary person. I never seem to have any ideas. I'm just not that creative." This is a mistaken belief. We have creativity inside of us. Some of us just haven't figured out how to unleash it yet. If we've never considered ourselves to be creative, this doesn't mean that we don't have the ability to be creative; it just means that we don't fully understanding the process of unleashing it.

Enhancing and unleashing personal creativity is fundamental to creating value. So understanding how to spark our creative side is a critical thing, unless we want to spend the rest of our lives building someone else's dream and living an inauthentic life. As a follow up work to his national bestseller *Flow*, Dr. Mihaly Csikszentmihalyi wrote *Creativity: Flow And The Psychology of Discovery and Invention.*[10] As part of the book, Dr. Csikszentmihalyi conducted over one hundred interviews with creative people from a broad cross selection of fields and incorporated the interviews into his vast research on the subject of flow psychology. The resultant work is a fascinating study of how flow theory can be used to bring clarity to the creative process.

Each person, Dr. Csikszentmihalyi believes, has the "potential" to lead a creative life, and tapping this creativity is an important aspect of one's fulfillment. He notes,

> Even though personal creativity may not lead to fame and fortune, it can do something that from the individual's point of view is even more important: make day to day experiences more vivid, more enjoyable, more rewarding. When we live creatively, boredom is banished and every moment holds the promise of a fresh discovery.[11]

10 Csikszentmihalyi, Mihaly, *Creativity: Flow And The Psychology Of Discovery And Invention.* New York: HarperCollins Publishers, 1996. Print.

11 Csikszentmihalyi, *Creativity*, 344.

There are however, four major obstacles to creativity. First, Dr. Csikszent-mihalyi notes many people are simply *"exhausted by too many demands."* As a result, they are not able to focus the psychic energy necessary to activate the creative aspects of their neurochemistry. Many people can relate to this first obstacle. It seems that despite the continual progress of technology, our lives continue to get cluttered and overcomplicated. Compound that with what seems to be a continual rising cost of living, and the societal pressures to "get ahead," "acquire the good things in life," and "save for retirement" and we have the context for a storm of psychic entropy. The pressure of continual demands is the enemy of mental focus, which in turn impedes our ability to tap creativity. This obstacle is understandably challenging, he notes:

> It is difficult to approach the world creatively when one is hungry or shivering from cold, because then all one's mental energy is focused on securing the necessities one lacks. And it is equally difficult when a person is rich and famous but devotes all of his or her energies to getting more money and fame. To free up creative energy we need to let go and divert some attention from the pursuit of the predictable goals that genes and memes have programmed in our minds and use it instead to explore the world around us on its own terms.[12]

The second obstacle preventing us from being creative is a close cousin to the first. Where there is "continual distraction" we have difficulty channeling creativity. This can take us out without much effort. The culprit: any form of social media and a smart phone. Facebook, Twitter, Instagram, LinkedIn, and Pinterest have wildly addictive propensities for distraction, and the distraction can be enjoyable. It is fun to see the pictures of our friend's vacation. It is fun to see the link shared by our buddy about someone else's dysfunctional life (especially if it is a celebrity). But these distractions are a death touch to creativity. In order to be creative we have to be able to focus, free from distraction.

The third obstacle to creativity is our often lack of ability to control the flow of our own energy. For some people this may also be just plain laziness. Many people don't understand how to channel their energy. This is a difficult one however, because in all fairness, we sometimes just get stuck in an "energy rut." We work long and hard hours in unfulfilling jobs. When we are

---

12   Csikszentmihalyi, Creativity, 346.

in our "off hours" we are tired. When we are tired we are not able to channel our creativity. In order to change this we may have to fundamentally alter some of our lifestyle habits (including our diet and our exercise routine). Or alternatively, we need to create a vision of what we want to pull us past fatigue and allow us to work into the late hours.

The final obstacle noted by Dr. Csikszentmihalyi is that many people don't have a clear vision for what they want out of life. They haven't determined what life is about for them, what their purpose is, or what life means to them. As a result, they don't really know what to do with the restless energy that they possess. Many will just fall into one of the ever-ready distractions, whether it be surfing the Internet or watching TV. Others will pass their time, and energy, pursuing a hobby that brings them a sense of contentment. There is absolutely nothing wrong with this; however it doesn't bring out their inner creative ability.

Now for a Solution: Do This if We Want to Tap Our Creative Genius

In *Creativity*, Dr. Csikszentmihalyi gives a "prescriptive" remedy to the person looking to break their current pattern and unleash their unique creativity. If a lack of creativity is something that we struggle with, and we're looking to really advance our own creative abilities, I would strongly encourage reading in detail his book and implementing the advice given. These steps have helped me to channel creativity in my business and writing. In essence his advice fits into four general categories. I will describe them as follows, step 1 to step 4:

Step 1: Become Like a Kid Again: Cultivate Curiosity

Children have a massive advantage over adults in the creative department. Their entire world is one of discovery, wonder and awe. Many adults, with age, lose their sense of wonder, and their sense of discovery about the world. Creative individuals are able however to maintain a habit of creativity throughout their life. The more curious we are, the more creative we'll be. That is what the research suggests. Dr. Csikszentmihalyi has some suggestions about how we can increase our curiosity. First, try to be surprised by something each day—don't assume that we have the whole world figured out—allow ourselves the freedom to be marveled. Next, try to surprise at least one person every day, do or say something unexpected. Breaking our own routine of behavior can actually trigger our creativity. Finally, take inventory of our discoveries and if something sparks our interest then follow it. Buy a book on it. Listen to a podcast about it. Do a little research about it on the Internet. All these things will unleash curiosity, which will facilitate creativity

Step 2: Learn to Cultivate Flow in Everyday Life

This step is important because it helps us to "enjoy" the process of being curious. Flow, as previously described, is the act of channeling all of our energy and focus in the pursuit of individually chosen and personally meaningful goals. When we do this we eliminate psychic entropy. These moments tend to be the most meaningful, or "optimal," in our life. However, if we don't have a goal that we are pursuing (or our goals are externally imposed and not meaningful to us personally) then our thoughts will eventually resort back to their default state of restlessness, entropy (and distraction), boredom or anxiety.

Dr. Csikszentmihalyi notes that we can channel flow by doing the following: first, wake up in the morning each day with a specific goal to look forward to. This is the art of "intentional living." Creative people wake up each day excited to create. They aren't drug out of bed. This is because they truly believe that what they are attempting to accomplish that day is creative and meaningful. If we think our life isn't meaningful then just start this habit by thinking of a single meaningful goal that we might accomplish in a day. Do this long enough and we'll be amazed at how our outlook changes.

The next method of channeling flow is to throw our whole self into what we do. If we do anything particularly well, that act will become more enjoyable to us. If we are enjoying it, we will facilitate creativity more naturally. As Dr. Csikszentmihalyi notes, "*whether writing a poem or cleaning the house, running a scientific experiment or a race, the quality of experience tends to improve in proportion to the effort invested in it.*[13] When we invest psychic energy into our self-directed goals, the activity becomes intrinsically rewarding. This means that the journey itself becomes the reward, not just the destination.

Creativity is channeled through flow by asking a simple question in each activity we engage in, "how can I apply flow conditions to this activity?" We are then forced to think about how a routine or mundane activity can be turned into a flow experience by channeling focus, setting a specific goal, and putting all our energy into the pursuit. This is powerful. As Dr. Csikszentmihalyi states:

> Eventually you will master the most important skill of all, the metaskill that consists in being able to turn any activity into an occasion of flow. If the autotelic metaskill is developed enough, you should be able to enjoy any new challenge and be on the way to the self-sustaining chain reaction of creativity.[14]

Finally, to keep things enjoyable we have to constantly seek increased complexity. In other words, we have to continually try to improve. This is fundamentally why creativity can lead to a lifetime of enjoyment. Creativity causes us to expand what we know and what we accept as settled. It causes us to look for new solutions to old problems. This is enjoyable. We cannot enjoy the same activity over and over again, unless there is an element of new challenges and new opportunities. Fundamental to the concept of flow is the concept of rising challenges to meet our ever-growing skill set.

Step 3: Develop Habits that Protect Our Energy and Our Ability to Focus

The third step in cultivating our creativity is to cultivate habits that protect our energy and our ability to focus. Dr. Csikszentmihalyi advises,

> We must erect barriers against distractions, dig channels so that energy can flow more freely, find ways to escape outside temptations and interruptions. If we do not, entropy is sure to break down the concentration that the pursuit of an inter-

---

13 Csikszentmihalyi, Creativity, 349.

14 Csikszentmihalyi, Creativity, 350.

est requires. Then thought returns to its baseline state—the vague, unfocused, constantly distracted condition of the normal mind.[15]

This step is really about taking control of our consciousness, and what our mind focuses on, and not allowing us to be distracted by things that aren't meaningful. There is a humorous side note to this principle concerning Steve Jobs and Albert Einstein. Both made conscious decisions to "eliminate choice" when it came to their daily wardrobe. For Jobs it meant only wearing black turtlenecks, jeans and sneakers. For Einstein it was baggy sweaters and slacks. Both men were said to have remarked that it was a conscious choice to free themselves from "having to think" about something that they considered meaningless.

So what can we do to build up habits to take control of our consciousness? Dr. Csikszentmihalyi suggests the following: first, take charge of our schedule. This can be difficult with work or other demands, but for some people our creative drive is best channeled early in the morning or late at night. So a mid-day nap may not be a bad thing (if possible). We have to figure out our own patterns of energy and shape our days to accommodate these patterns. Next, we have to ensure proper time is allocated to reflection and relaxation. Being constantly busy is not a good recipe for creativity. As the eastern proverb goes, *when the mind is clear inspiration often follows*.

Additionally we need to shape our space. Our surroundings can have a critical impact on our creativity. On a micro level this would extend to our "creative workspace" or office. Do we have one? It may also mean a change in where we live. Some people are highly sensitive to sun depravation, or feeling crowded in an urban center. This is something to seriously consider. We may feel "trapped" in an area right now, but it is a real shame to go our entire life without tapping our creativity, when a simple move could stimulate our creative abilities.

The final suggestion in this step is one that I have written on at length in this book. It is to find out who we really are. Find out what we like and what we don't like. Determine with clarity what we value. There is only one of us. We need to know what that "us" consists of. Then, most importantly,

15 Csikszentmihalyi, Creativity, 351.

we need to have the courage to do more of what we value, and less of what we don't, regardless of what anyone says. It seems so simple, but it's so often neglected in practice. However, it is very clear that the more we do things that we like, and the less we do things that we don't like, the more creative we will be.

Step 4: Internalize What We've Learned into Our Personality and Seek Complexity

Step four is really about incorporating steps one through three into our personality, in other words our *"habitual way of thinking, feeling, and acting, as the more or less unique pattern by which we use psychic energy or attention."*[16] It can be very difficult to change our personality. Not only is it the product of years of socialization and habit, but it is also genetically imprinted on us as well. However, we are capable of changing and adapting our personality to one that is more closely aligned with the personalities of creative people. To this end Dr. Csikszentmihalyi gives three suggestions.

First, we must be constantly willing to develop in areas that we are lacking. Creativity is channeled through personality development:

> The point here is that everyone can strengthen the missing end of the polarity. When an extrovert learns to experience the world like an introvert, or vice versa, it is as if he or she discovered a whole missing dimension to the world...In all of these cases, a new realm of experience opens up in front of us, which means that in effect we double and then double again the content of life.[17]

When we double the experience and content of our life our mind is opened up to the possibilities of what we were missing in a closed view. This motivates us to continually open the realms of our consciousness to discover new possibilities. This process is the process of creativity.

Next, we need to shift often from openness to closure. Creative people, Dr. Csikszentmihalyi notes, have the uncanny paradoxical ability to be open and receptive at times, but stubborn in their worldviews, at others. They are able to shift between two perspectives easily and effortlessly. They know

---

16 Csikszentmihalyi, *Creativity*, 358.

17 Csikszentmihalyi, *Creativity*, 360.

when they should be open to further discovery and perhaps outside interpretation or assistance, and they also know when they need to pursue what
they know in their heart to be correct, even if others disagree. Our ability to
experience both mindsets doubles the experience of life and makes it possible to find creativity at both poles.

Finally, a creative personality will continually seek complexity. A continual desire for complexity necessitates a creative outlook. We cannot increase
the complexity of any act, environment, relationship or endeavor unless we
are creative enough to think outside of our current setting into a new possibility of what could be. Complexity is rooted in an understanding of what
currently is, and the prospect of what the future could hold. The first form
of complexity that everyone should seek out is the continual complexity of
the self. As Dr. Csikszentmihalyi notes, *"by fully expressing the tendencies of
which we are capable, we become part of the energy that creates the future.."*[18]

Channeling Negative Energy into Uninhibited Creativity: The Whiteboard

All of us have felt and will continue to feel pain. We all encounter negative
energy. It is impossible to completely avoid it. It comes in many different,
and unexpected forms. Sometimes people, who we consider friends, will
say and do hurtful things to us. They do these things because they are not
happy with themselves; nevertheless, their actions sting. All of us encounter
rejection, failure and setbacks, especially if we are chasing difficult goals and
confronting fears. It is very hard to put into full application the principles of
accepting failure as education, detachment and the other concepts discussed
in this book. We have realistic fears and anxieties that will continue to rear
their disempowering head, no matter how proactive we become, and no
matter how far down the path of our dreams we may be travelling.

Negativity is unmistakably "energy," but it doesn't have to be negative.
If we allow it to be negative it will many times manifest itself in the form of
anger, jealousy or fear. Anger is a powerful emotion that can catalyze action.
Often however the action is to fight back, seek retribution, spread hurt, or

18 Csikszentmihalyi, Creativity, 363.

lash out. However, this is disempowering. There is a better way to deal with these emotions. Instead of letting negativity transform into anger, we can use the emotions of defeat, pain, fear, anxiety, or anger to stimulate wild, uninhibited creativity.

I have a blank whiteboard that sits very close to me in my office. It is my friend because it is the primary tool that allows me to channel any anger, fear, pain or anxiety that I may periodically feel into wild, uninhibited creativity. Whenever I get angry, whenever I get hurt, whenever someone says or does something that I interpret as unfair or insensitive I go to my whiteboard and I create. I create new goals. I create plans to achieve those goals. I create innovative ideas, strategies and techniques to succeed in my business and in my life. I create. When I first left law to build a business with my wife, people who didn't understand my decision criticized me. Instead of getting angry I simply used my whiteboard to channel my creativity.

Every time I feel that I can't accomplish what I want to, I go back to the board. I start to write. I start to create. Creativity soon follows. I have learned that anger, or any negative emotion will actually ignite my creative drive if I have the right conduit to transform it. When I channel negativity I become wildly creative, and guess what, by the time I am done creating, I am no longer angry. Funny isn't it?

In Order to Tap Our Inner Greatness We Need to Attempt Difficult Things

If we want to tap our inner greatness, unleash our wild creativity into the world, and add unique value to others, we have to be willing to attempt difficult things, particularly things that we aren't initially good at. Even if we fail repeatedly, we need the mental toughness to try again. Nothing develops mental toughness better than trying difficult things, regardless of the outcome. I really believe this. For me, my most recent example of this principle is Brazilian Jiu-Jitsu. I'm not adept; in fact, I've found the martial art to feel quite unnatural and difficult. I'm not that flexible. I'm not a "tough guy." I'm pretty friendly. I'm built more like a runner than a fighter.

Whenever I go to the local Gracie Barra that I train at, I repeatedly get tapped. I get tangled. I get tied into a human pretzel and I can't breathe. I come home sore and many times bruised. It is so crazy, but it feels so great.

Every time I attend a class I really come home feeling great about myself. I have pondered why this is the case. I have wondered why, when I am doing something that is not comfortable or natural, after the event (even though there is often pain involved), I come home feeling great. I think I have some answers.

We live in a world where we are constantly and consciously trying to eliminate pain and difficulty. We actually become paranoid about "experiencing" anything that will potentially hurt us. But pain has its place. It makes us strong. It makes us brave. It gives us a reference point for what we can and can't tolerate. If we didn't experience pain we couldn't grow. In many cases I am amazed at just how much I can actually endure. When I realize this I feel great about myself, and I realize that regardless of the outcome, I am mentally strong.

Every time I do something that I am scared of, after I actually do it, I come out with a much greater sense of self. I feel like I have secured a victory. I obtain a victory every time I go. I obtain the victory of myself over myself. I have defeated my fear. This makes me feel great. When we aren't very good at something, we can only improve. We are already at the bottom. We are already the worst. So we have nothing to prove. We have nothing to lose. Everything is a gain. When we realize this, each experience becomes enjoyable because we are learning; we are making progress (even if that progress is very slow).

Doing difficult things, particularly things we aren't good at, eliminates the negative components of our ego. This is one of the most enjoyable things in life. Our ego is our "chimpanzee brain." It is what triggers jealously, unhappiness and anxiety in our life. When we are being beat up (literally or metaphorically), in an activity that is hard, we can't have an ego. Our ego is gone. When this happens we are in a wonderful place. We wonder why we ever had an ego in the first place. We realize what a liability our ego has always been. When we attempt difficult things we realize that we want to attempt more. Then our life starts to expand. We get adventurous. We get curious.

Checkpoint:
How to Channel Our Creative Genius

1. Become like a kid again; cultivate curiosity in all that we do.

2. Learn to cultivate flow in our everyday life.

3. Develop habits that protect our energy and our ability to focus.

4. Internalize what we've learned into our personality and seek complexity.

5. Channel negative energy into an uninhibited creative expression.

6. Do difficult things, even (especially) if they expand our comfort zone.

What All This Is Ultimately About: Happiness

I have been unhappy at times in my life. I have been down right depressed. I have no fear in admitting it and I've discussed it in detail in this book. For me, my depression peaked with my stark realization that I had spent years of my life, and hundreds of thousands of dollars, training myself for a career that I didn't want to do. Since that time my life has changed immensely. I have transformed myself from a cynical, pessimistic, and unhappy person to one that is naturally upbeat, energetic, full of positive engagement, and happy. My wife and I have built a wonderful business. It has given me clarity, hope and purpose. We have time as a family to enjoy each other. I have time to pursue goals that are personally meaningful and intrinsically fulfilling.

How did I do it? I want to share some discoveries, and the resulting "rules" that I have adopted. I do this sincerely to help whoever might read this book. I know exactly what it feels like to not want to get out of bed, to have random waves of debilitating anxiety, fear, and sadness, and to feel like life is meaningless. I've been there. I also know that when we are able to tap our true self, when we are able to live life fully and happily, we are able to add value to others. This is the key to success in today's economy.

I'm not so arrogant, or ignorant, to think that my "rules" are some sort of a universal constitution applicable to all people. Nor for that matter do I necessarily believe that my rules will actually work on everyone. Fundamental to what I believe (and what I have discussed in detail throughout this book) is that our core values have to match our actions and goals. My rules are based on what I value.

I believe that everyone must discover what makes them happy on their own. We can't adopt someone else's method. It is just too personal. There are many books that tell us "how to be happy." I have read a good chunk of them. Oddly enough I discovered my rules on my own. They just came to me, independent on any book or "guru." As they came to me, I knew that they were correct, for me. I live by an edict from Ralph Waldo Emerson's Essay on Self-Reliance:

> There is a time in every man's education when he arrives at the conviction that envy is ignorance; that imitation is suicide….Trust thyself: every heart vibrates to that iron string.[19]

So I'm not looking to give anyone answers. I'm not looking to be a guru. But in the slight positive chance that my rules do help in any way, I want to share them. I simply want to share my rules because being unhappy is no way to live, and also because contributing to others is one of my core values. If even one rule works, that is a good thing.

It will be easy to notice that nowhere in my rules will we find anything about worldly success. It's an interesting observation that I've made. Without a doubt in my mind, I believe that happiness doesn't come by acquisition of title, achievement or attainment of money or "stuff." These are the idols that I sought early in my life, and my pursuit didn't bring me happiness. Happiness isn't "arrived at." It is a process. I also believe that happiness doesn't come from our attained "status" in relation to others, or from the

---

19 Emerson, Ralph Waldo, *Self-Reliance*. New York: Do You Zoom, Inc., 2011. Print

opinions of others. Again, just my opinion, but without a doubt, focusing on "stuff," being obsessed about getting a certain "amount" of money in our bank account, or "impressing others" has never made me happy.

I came up with my rules through reading and my own self-directed experiments. I would research what had worked for other people, and I would then apply them to my life to see if they worked for me. This research process helped me determine what for me was useful. I think this process alone was one of my greatest discoveries. Not everything that works for other people necessarily works for me, and I needed to preserve my own intellect, and make my own discoveries and my own decisions. So, in no particular order, here are my "10 Rules For Being Happy."

Rule 1: I Need to Make Sure that I'm Internally Aligned

I need inner congruency, in that my goals, and the way that I spend my time must be in line with the things that I value most. I value freedom, positive contribution to others, adventure and curiosity, education, good health and rich relationships, particularly family, personal growth and continued complexity. In order for me to be happy, my goals, and daily actions must be directed at pursuing endeavors that facilitate these core values.

In law I had no freedom, literally almost a complete absence of it. I rarely felt like I was truly adding value to the world, or that I was growing personally. I didn't get to travel and experience adventure. I hardly had any time to stay healthy. Yes I had to learn, but it wasn't in areas that interested me, and I felt that the learning was compelled, it didn't feel self directed. I wasn't forging lasting friendships. Most importantly, in order to succeed in law I had to spend more time away from my family. No wonder I was unhappy.

Rule 2: I Need to Live by the "Magical Question"

The magical question is, "what is the most amazing, fun and wild thing that could happen in my life in the next [insert time period]?" The answer to this question becomes my primary focus for that corresponding time period. This exercise is just plain fun. It's what gets me excited. It's what gets me out of bed and keeps me awake at night—the magical question. I love being

crazy with it—thinking of wild and outrageous things. Then giving everything I have to make it happen. For some reason (that I can't explain), this
just really, really excites me.

Rule 3: When I'm Pursuing the Magical Question I Need to Push Myself to the Absolute Best that Is in Me

For another interesting reason that I can't fully explain, I know that when I
am pushing myself to the absolute best that is within, I feel more alive than
ever. I think it might have something to do with flow psychology. I'm not
sure. I just know that it works. I am absolutely most alive, and happy, when
I am pushing myself as hard as I possibly can to pursue the magical question. Whatever I pursue, I must give my best in it. That is a precondition for
happiness for me.

Rule 4: If Something Scares Me, I Need to Move Towards It

I believe this works because when I move forward in the face of fear, I am
becoming a more complex individual. I am growing, and growth feels good.
If I get scared of something, and I move towards it, if attempt it, and embrace it, I will be happy. I think it is also because of the signal my brain gets
when overcoming a fear or an obstacle. It must be biological, but the reality
is that I just know that it works. If I'm scared of something I should move
towards it. I should try it, whatever it is. By moving towards my fears my life
becomes rich and full. When my life becomes rich and full, I am happier.

Rule 5: I Need to be Present in What I Do, Especially When It Comes to Relationships

This is one where technology does us in. iPhones, Androids, BlackBerrys,
Smartphones—they kill (or at least seriously impede) our ability to stay present. I am guilty of this all the time (although I am constantly working on it),
being with someone but not being fully present. I have found that, without
a doubt, I enjoy the conversation and the relationship much more if I am
present. I enjoy everything I do much more if I am present. This principle
applies to so much: driving the car, mowing the lawn, hanging out with my

kids, and doing marketing for my business. Whatever I do, I will enjoy it more if I am present.

Rule 6: Learning and Reading Makes Me Happy, So I Need to Make Sure I Never Stop

I am an absolute book junkie. I love reading. I love learning. I am one of www.audible.com's most loyal customers. I religiously listen to podcasts on topics of business, science, philosophy and religion. I am a learning junkie. This makes me happy. I can never stop learning. I am a lifelong learner.

Rule 7: Being In Good General Health Has a Direct Impact On My Emotional State

This one is a no-brainer, but hard for many to put into action. When I am exercising and eating healthy I feel better and I am more confident. When I feel better, and have more confidence, I am happier. When I eat poorly, fail to exercise, and do not take care of myself I do not feel as good. This is a simple equation in my life.

Rule 8: The First Great Paradox: I Desire Rich Relationships, But I Cannot be Worried about What Others Think of Me

A sure fire recipe for being unhappy, absolutely 100% guaranteed in my opinion, is to constantly try to please other people, and to become overly concerned with other's opinions. It just doesn't work, and it makes us miserable in the process. If we are overly concerned with other people's opinions, we will not take risks, we will not allow ourselves to be vulnerable, we will not go out of our comfort zone, and we will not fully live. I have found that there is a strong positive correlation between my willingness to take risks, be vulnerable and go outside of my comfort zone and my happiness. The more vulnerable I get, the happier I am.

We have to be ourselves, and there is only one of us. No matter how quirky we are. No matter if our interests are strange. If we feel like dancing then we should dance, even, in fact especially, if we have no rhythm. If we've never felt what it feels like to dance like we swallowed a monkey and that monkey is going crazy inside of us then, in my opinion, we are missing out on one of the great happy experiences in life.

The first great paradox is that I believe we need people to be complete. But it is most often another person that contributes to our periods of unhappiness. Here is how I have learned to balance these competing principles. I am just myself. By being myself I will draw certain people to me. The people that I draw to me will be my lifelong friends and they will fulfill my need for deep relationships. I will also unintentionally push some people away. If I want to be truly happy then I have to be ok with that result. I have to just be me. I have to own it, rock it, and embrace it, even if I am different, and even if my "choice" of career isn't someone else's choice of a career. I cannot be happy if I am constantly concerned about impressing others, or seeking their approval.

If we master this principle we will become immune to worrying about failure. Failure only has the meaning that we give to it. Failure could just as easily be termed "education" or "growth." Don't all scientists technically fail when conducting experiments if they don't get the result they want on the first try? Does that stop the scientist from trying again? Of course not! But so many people fail to apply scientific logic to their life. We are only worried about failure if we are worried about other's opinions. The moment we stop caring about the opinions of others we are no longer afraid of failure. When we are no longer afraid of failure we are in a powerful personal position, and, we are happier.

Rule 9: The Second Great Paradox: Although I Attack My Goals with Passion, I Must also Detach from the Results and Enjoy the Ride

This is a really hard one to put into practice as well. It is hard because we actually "want" our results, otherwise we wouldn't set a goal. But this is the principle where the cliché "the journey is the destination" isn't a cliché. It is an absolute truth that must be applied if we are to be happy. I have learned that sometimes, no matter what we do, we can't control the outcome. So if we become fixated on an outcome, and we create an internal "rule" that says we will only be satisfied if we get this outcome, and then something out of our control happens that prevents us from getting the outcome, we will often be unhappy.

In order to be truly happy in life we have to learn to enjoy the ride. If we live constantly in the future our life will pass us by. If we are fixated on "rewards" alone, but live a miserable day-to-day experience, we will soon come to realize that life is just the sum of our day-to-day experiences. Learning to lose ourself in the process of achieving a goal is extremely rewarding.

I learned this lesson when I played basketball in college. The more I became fixated with scoring points, the less I actually enjoyed playing, and strangely enough, the worse I performed. The more I lost myself in the moment of the game, the more I fully immersed myself in everything I was doing, the more I enjoyed the game, and strangely enough, the better I performed. This principle has its roots in flow psychology, in eastern religious traditions such as Zen, and also in texts such as the *Bhagavad Gita*. Life, at least for me, is truly most enjoyable when I am appreciating the ride, when I am pursuing a fun goal (the magical question), but I don't get so fixated on the rewards that the journey itself becomes less desirable. Also, equally as important, if I am fixated on the reward I can become risk intolerant. I become scared of failure. If I detach, then I am willing to swing for the fence. I have nothing to lose. Paradoxically, this is needed if we want big results.

The way this rule plays out in application is that it is easy to enjoy the ride when we are setting fun goals. If our goals are not inspiring, exciting, fun or imaginative then it can be much more difficult to enjoy the ride. Again this is a very hard principle to put into application. "Detaching" is not an easy thing to do, especially in our consumer driven culture.

Rule 10: Life Is a Great Experiment, a Curious Discovery, a Thousand Simple Tests

This is my "I'm a kid again," or "I'm a great amateur inventor" or "I'm a mad scientist" or "I'm a wizard making spells" principle. This principle is the ultimate protection from failure. There can be no such thing as failure because everything is an experiment. Actions lead to results. If my actions don't lead to the results that I want, then I simply change my actions. This is perhaps the greatest discovery of them all. Failure is a made up concept. It has no meaning to me.

I am on a path of discovery. Life is grand. I'm like a kid, seeing a butterfly for the first time and chasing it through the grass. If something looks interesting to me, I try it. If I don't want to do it anymore, I don't. When we live this way we have serious control of our emotional state. This principle applied doesn't mean that we are non-committal. Quite the opposite, we are deeply committed to our core values. It just means that we aren't going to get bogged down in the silly game of "comparison" with other people. Our life is our own. It doesn't matter what other people do or what other people have. If it resonates true with us, then it is good. We should pursue it and make life our grand experiment. Treat life like my favorite Henry David Thoreau quote (as previously mentioned):

> I wished to live deliberately, to front only the essential facts of life, and see if I could not learn what it had to teach, and not, when I came to die, discover that I had not lived. I did not wish to live what was not life, living is so dear; nor did I wish to practice resignation, unless it were quite necessary. I wanted to live deep and suck all the marrow out of life.[20]

My rules allow me to live deeply. They make life meaningful and rich. I hope we all can define our own unique rules. Life is too dear not to live it deeply. Life is too short not to be happy.

---

20 Thoreau, 74.

Checkpoint:
My 10 Rules for Being Happy

1. I need to make sure that I'm internally aligned.

2. I need to live by the "magical question."

3. When I'm pursuing the magical question I need to push myself to the absolute best that is in me.

4. If something scares me, I need to move towards it.

5. I need to be present in what I do, especially when it comes to relationships.

6. Learning and reading makes me happy, so I need to make sure I never stop.

7. Being in good general health has a direct impact on my emotional state.

8. The first great paradox: I desire rich relationships, but I cannot be worried about what others think of me.

9. The second great paradox: although I attack my goals with passion, I must also detach from the results and enjoy the ride.

10. Life is a great experiment, a curious discovery, a thousand simple tests.

Beginning the Rest of Our Lives

Just Start: Our New Life Begins with a Real Decision and a Commitment to Work

Everything in life starts with a decision: the decision to enter into a relationship or have kids, the decision to start a business, the decision to change careers, the decision to stop being a victim, stop blaming others or external factors, and take 100% responsibility for our emotional well-being. A great song was preceded by the decision to sit down and compose, even if it began as an improvisation, there was that flicker of a moment to begin to compose. For every painting or piece of art, a decision was first made to walk to the blank canvas. Every book started with the decision to sit down and write, and then keep writing until it was done. We make a decision when we begin to "do." Everything starts with a decision: our new life, our new career, and our sense of fulfillment and purpose must first start with a decision.

Decisions are the mechanism that facilitates ideas into tangible existence. Everything first begins in the mind, in the form of a thought, but it takes a decision, backed by discipline to move that thought into reality. Many people have ideas. Many people think about working from home or abroad, starting a business, writing a book, starting a blog, or attempting something unique, but it seems that only a few people actually pull it off. A true decision involves removing the escape route. The etymology of the word "decide" suggests "cutting off" alternatives. So in actuality many people fail to create, they fail to start, they fail to take a chance because they fail to decide, in that they fail to make a true decision, a decision where alternatives are eliminated. When they fail to decide they miss out on the feelings of being alive that are associated with taking risks, and charting our own unique course.

What is the force that prevents people from stepping over the threshold and making real decisions, regardless of the consequences? One of my favorite writers, Steven Pressfield in his books *The War of Art: Break Through The Blocks And Win Your Inner Creative Battles*[1] and *Turning Pro: Tap Your Inner Power And Create Your Life's Work*[2], labels this pernicious force "resistance." Resistance can take many forms: fear, laziness, distraction, addiction, indulgence, self-doubt, or listening to the critics. It can be subtle, and embody what Pressfield calls "shadow careers," where we are too scared to seek out our true calling (even through we know deep down in our hearts what that calling is) so instead we pursue a shadow career, one that really entails no real risk, and one that if we fail, the consequences are basically meaningless.[3] For me, law was a shadow career.

Resistance is a terribly effective force. It invokes paralysis, rationalization and immobilization. It justifies fear by distorting the importance of "being rational" when in reality sometimes the very best thing that could ever happen to us is that we take an irrational position, indulge a risky venture or an "unorthodox" career move. Resistance, as Pressfield notes, will catch us dead in our tracks. Resistance always rears its ugly head when a creative endeavor is attempted, and don't for one second think that starting a business isn't a creative endeavor. Resistance has stopped, and will continue to stop, many people from creating their art, whatever that art may be.

How do we stop this paralyzing force? Pressfield's answer has literally changed my life. We defeat resistance by doing our work. We defeat resis-

---

1   Pressfield, Steven, *The War of Art: Break Through The Blocks And Win Your Inner Creative Battles.* New York: Black Irish Entertainment LLC, 2012. Print.

2   Pressfield, Steven, *Turning Pro: Tap Your Inner Power And Create Your Life's Work.* New York: Black Irish Entertainment LLC, 2012. Print.

3   Pressfield, Turning Pro, 13.

tance by being a professional. What does this mean? It means that if we make the decision that we are going to leave our current career because our heart is calling us elsewhere, we make the decision, and then we stop thinking about it. We control the fear and the criticism through work, plain and simple. Work keeps the mind from stirring. Work keeps the anxieties from racing. Work keeps fear from being immobilizing. We sit down and we work. As Pressfield once noted on his blog, *"you put your ass where you heart wants to be."* There is no other path. This is the path of the professional: work.

If our heart is yearning for freedom from our nine to five, then in the hours from when the kids go to bed, until we can't keep our eyes open anymore from fatigue, we must be building our business. Resistance will take the form of the TV and surfing the Internet. Resistance will take the form of making us believe that our idea won't turn a profit. It will take the form of self-hypnosis that we don't have what it takes to market ourselves. We shut up resistance through work. That is what a pro does. A pro doesn't spend her life in self-analysis. A pro spends her life refining her craft.

Defeating resistance is how I wrote this book—day after day after day. I had many self-doubts. I still do, "what do I have to say?" "who wants to read this anyway?" "I am too busy with our business," but my heart kept yearning, so I knew that it was something I needed to finish. Every time I felt resistance I would immediately make a goal to push out another 500 words, then another 500 words, then another, until finally the book was completed. Whether or not this book is beneficial, or even effectively written, isn't what is most important to me. What is most important to me is that I defeated resistance. I had a thought in my head and a purpose to write. I had a message that I wanted to share because I knew that it could help others, so I kept at it. I kept working until the message was out. I defeated resistance. That was my goal. Anything else is ancillary. The most important rewards for me are the ones that are experienced internally.

That is the way that we take the ideas in this book and bring them into reality. If we want to write a book, learn a language, get a purple belt in Jiu-Jitsu, start a business, figure out how to make passive income on the Internet, weed our garden, anything, there is only one path: work. We need Spartan-like discipline to sit down every singe day and make progress. When resistance rears its ugly head we defeat it by doing our work. We work on our business every single day. We work on unleashing our creativity every single day. This process is at the heart of my rules for being happy. I can trace everything positive that has happened in my life since I left law to this process: first, discovering what I value, what makes me tick, what makes me feel alive, outside of any monetary goal or social status; second, making a true decision to pursue it, this means actually cutting off alternatives; and third, defeating resistance each day by showing up and doing my work.

This process makes the journey fulfilling. It is freeing because my life is no longer about the rewards. It is about the process. The process in and of itself is fulfilling. It is autotelic. It is self-contained. Life is most rewarding, most rich and most abundant when each day I am defeating resistance on the path of what I value most. This is the path of ultimate freedom. It is the freedom of the mind. I am free from the trap of external rewards or seeking money goals just because that is what everyone else is doing. I am free from the trap of needing other's approval or acclaim to make myself feel complete. Life is no longer a competition where money is the score, or where what my neighbor does, or buys, impacts my thoughts. Life is my own to experience. It is about doing the work that I know I was meant to do. It is about fulfilling my own unique purpose. Empowerment is about finding our unique purpose, by guiding our own destiny, writing our own story. This is my purpose, and by my own empowerment, I am able to facilitate the empowerment of those I love, my tribe, and serve for the betterment of our society as a whole.

Checkpoint: Just Start

✓ Our new life begins with a decision, and then intentional and sustained action.

✓ A true decision involves cutting off alternatives.

✓ Day in day out, one step at a time, is how we will create the life we truly value.

✓ Any courageous endeavor meets resistance. We defeat resistance through work.

✓ Ultimately, our work is all that matters.

✓ Work mitigates fear, causes anxiety to subside, and channels creativity.

✓ Start today to define, and build, the life you really want.

✓ By empowering ourselves, we give others permission to succeed, we inspire and empower others.

CPSIA information can be obtained
at www.ICGtesting.com
Printed in the USA
LVOW13s2355061017
551545LV00015B/642/P